THE LADDER OR THE GRIND

Jonathan Patrick

Jonathan Patrick

www.jonathanmillspatrick.com

First Edition: January 2020

Publisher is not responsible for websites (or their content) that are not owned by the publisher.

ISBN: 9798606608119

This book is dedicated to my father. You set the tone for the business professional that I aimed to be.

Contents

Foreword

If you search online for information about going from an employee to an entrepreneur you won't lack for content. Switch that around, look for guides on going from being an entrepreneur to an employee, and you might find nothing on the topic.

There are plenty of possible explanations for such a result. What I see as highest among those explanations is that it isn't cool to talk about becoming an employee. But the business world sure sees entrepreneurship as sexy as hell.

Just look at the number of books, movies, and TV shows that are based on the entrepreneurial endeavor. Shows like Shark Tank and The Profit, while certainly mentioning the struggle entrepreneurs go through, also glamorize running your own business.

There are thousands upon thousands of websites that provide resources dedicated to "escaping the 9 to 5" or becoming a "digital nomad".

However, the aggrandizement of being an employee rarely exists. Instead, there are shows like The Office or movies like Office Space where being an employee is portrayed as akin to being in prison.

Now, you might already be thinking that this book is going to be about why being an employee is better than being an entrepreneur. If so, you would be wrong. Dead wrong. But I am also not here to convince you that entrepreneurship is the way to go.

The real reason I wrote this book is to uncover the answer to that question for myself. Which question? Whether being an employee or being an entrepreneur is better for me?

The truth is that I have debated whether or not entrepreneurship or being an employee is right for me for a very, very long. You see, I've been both. I've even been both at the same time. I've been an employee of companies where I was the low man on the organizational chart and I've been at the top of the organizational chart at a $300,000,000 company. I've also been an entrepreneur through multiple endeavors. Some of those endeavors were successful and others were a complete failure. I've even written about that failure. Employee and freelancer at the same time? Check.

As I write this I have just finished an interview process where I would be a C-level executive at a $1.2 billion-dollar company. I went into that interview convinced it was time to give up on my entrepreneurial pursuits and go back to what I know, which is the finance world. After all, the compensation package at that company would be enough for me to retire in a few years.

But, if I am being honest, yesterday's interview left me unsure of whether or not that company is right for me. That is partly because of some of the negative inner dynamics that I uncovered. But also because I wasn't sure I would make a good employee after having largely autonomous for the past three-and-one-half years.

This isn't a debate that I take lightly. Whether my professional career skews back toward a corporate job or I continue my entrepreneurial journey largely depends on the research that I am doing for this book. But I am not just writing this book as a career exercise for myself. Because I know beyond a shadow of a doubt that there are a lot of people who have dreams of running their own business instead of "working for the man". But I am not sure they know what they are getting themselves into. As the saying goes, be careful what you wish for 'cause you just might get it all. Those people need to understand what comes with being an entrepreneur.

I can tell you that in the last week I have talked to a young man who is a first-time entrepreneur and is convinced he will never work for someone else again. I've also talked with a lifetime entrepreneur who admitted to me that she was ready for a corporate job with benefits. There are people on both sides of the fence. It's just that you don't hear about it.

My goal with this book is to provide you with information so that you can make an informed decision about your professional life. Whether you are a new college graduate looking for your first "real job" or an experienced entrepreneur who is burnt out, I want you to fully understand the positives and the negatives of both paths - employee or entrepreneur.

Or, as I think about that decision — climb the corporate ladder (The Ladder) as an employee or experience the entrepreneurial grind (The Grind).

The Ladder or The Grind

My professional career has been called eclectic before. I've even been accused of "dabbling" in businesses. Heck, I even called myself a dabbler in an interview with Tom Ballard of Teknovation. All of those statements are true.

The more time I have spent in self-development the more I realize that I have a unique set of professional experience and skills that have allowed me to explore and largely excel in a variety of roles in the business world. For example, there aren't a lot of professionals that have a blend of marketing and finance experience that I have. The two topics just don't normally fit together for most people.

But for me, they have worked well together. Those skills have allowed me to work with companies ranging from true startups to Fortune 30 tech giants. Using my finance experience I have also helped entrepreneurs raise over $500,000,000 in funding for their projects.

However, that breadth of experience has come with a cost. It has left me completely unsure of where I fit with the business ecosystem by leaving me feeling professionally trapped somewhere between being an employee and being an entrepreneur.

Which is exactly why I wanted to write this book in the first place.

I started the research process for this book with the belief that I would be able to get enough answers to my questions and enough supporting data to help me make a decision once and for all which career path was better for me. Because I was tired of being stuck in the middle of the two paths. I desperately wanted to answer one fundamental question - would I be happier climbing the corporate ladder (again) or in the grind that is called entrepreneurship?

Of course, I hoped that the findings I uncovered along the way would help you as well. I knew that I couldn't be the only person who is constantly asking themselves which path is best.

After all, I know plenty of people who are climbing the corporate ladder that dream of running their own business or founding the next high-growth startup. I talk to those kinds of people on an almost weekly basis. Most of them call me looking for funding for their projects. They have been smitten by the idea of entrepreneurship and are ready to claim their fortune. They just aren't sure where to get started. So, I spent a lot of time with those folks talking about their day jobs and why they wanted to be an entrepreneur. Plus, I pushed them to uncover and share what was holding them back from such dreams.

On the flip side of that coin, I thought that finding people who are entrepreneurs that just wanted to call it quits would be harder. But they do exist. More of them existed than I realized at the onset of this project. At one point I talked to about five people in the span of a few days who were done with running their own business. They had flat out had it with the hustle and grind and just wanted out. They were tired of every piece of their business being their responsibility. They were fleeing toward what they saw as more security and/or less time grinding away at a business that was never going to be more than a replacement for a typical job.

What I suspected was that the constant tug and pull of this question was going on behind the scenes of people's professional lives. Partially because they didn't know how to answer the question themselves or maybe they were just too scared to make a decision. Maybe they wanted to start their own business but they were scared of not having health insurance. Maybe some entrepreneurs wanted to re-enter the corporate world because they just wanted to work their 9-5 and then be able to shut their work out of their mind for the rest of the day.

To uncover the answers I knew that I was going to have to talk to the right people and then ask them some really hard questions. Questions that they would be willing to answer with complete honesty. Because, if we are being truthful, few people want to openly admit that they couldn't cut it as a business owner. That they sought the "safety" of a day job because the burden of being an entrepreneur was just too much. Others, that are employees, weren't likely to admit that they were happy with what they do. I mean, how many people have you talked to that has ever told you that they love their job? I can't count on two hands the number of people I have met that would say as much.

So, I started putting together the questions I wanted to be answered. Then I started reaching out to professionals that I knew that were employees and love it, that were entrepreneurs who would "never work for someone else again," and folks who were in the middle like me.

The result was some amazing interviews with some of the smartest and most candid people on earth. Not only were they willing to share their professional aspirations and stories, but our time together talking about this topic of career choices ended up often crossing into their personal lives. The best part is that in many of the interviews I realized that there was a point where I was no longer the person benefitting from the process. That by answering the questions I had about career paths and sharing their own choices each person ended up learning a lot about themselves and their professional journey. Without fail we would end the call with a discussion about how the interviewee was going to pursue some level of entrepreneurship or how they now viewed their corporate job in a much more favorable light.

I've written this book to intentionally be a mix of both facts and opinions. So, keep that in mind as you are reading through it. I choose that kind of mix because I wanted to avoid being too academic and boring you with too many charts full of statistics. But, I thought that kind of data was important enough to share it when it was valuable to take note of. At the same time, as a marketer at heart, I know the power of storytelling. That is why along the way many of the sections in the book will include my own story that is relevant to that section or a story I uncovered in my interviews or research.

By the way, you can watch the videos of those interviews at jonathanmillspatrick.com/theladderorthegrind/.

I can't thank you enough for your interest in this topic and this book. If you find any value in it please pay it forward and share it with a family member, friend, co-worker, or even a random stranger.

Because what started as a purely selfish project to help me answer my career questions ended up being a project that I knew would change how people looked at the career choices they made. I couldn't ask for a better result. Because, at the end of the day, if what follows in this book helps just one person pursue a career and life that leaves them happier, healthier, and better informed about the things to consider when choosing which professional life to pursue then it was worth it.

What's the Big Deal?

Why is this decision, whether or not you are better off as an employee or an entrepreneur, such a big deal in the first place? What is it about a person's profession that makes it such a huge piece of their life and such a critical part of their happiness?

A large part of that derives from the fact that even as young kids we are taught to think about what we want to be when we grow up. This starts very early in school. I can distinctly remember our daughter sharing, via video, that she wanted to be an artist. That was at her kindergarten graduation! What six-year-old has a clue about what they want to be when they grow up?

The pressure to put a stake in the ground about your profession of choice never lets up from there. It might wain a bit in middle school. But by the time students are in high school they are being taught to think about the next step. Heck, they are being taught to think multiple steps ahead. High school counselors teach students to start building a resume that will get them accepted into their college of choice. The focus is mostly on grades, but it is also on extra-curricular activities to make your admissions application stand out. Even the college students choose is part of this professional chess game all played to hopefully land you in the profession of your dreams.

There are multiple problems with this whole routine.

First, we are asking young people to make a decision that could impact them for the rest of their lives. That decision isn't based on a whole lot of information other than interests and aptitude. But interests change as people get older. I know they did for me. I wanted to teach martial arts when I was in middle school and that ended up being my first full-time job after graduating from college. But after a few years, I realized that my interest in that industry just wasn't there anymore. I wanted to do something more "professional". Almost twenty years after that professional pivot I am now more interested in work that is less "professional". People's interests change and so can their aptitude for certain subjects.

Second, almost every graduating senior I have mentored has based their career choices on the wrong thing. What thing is that? How much money they can make.

Now listen, I'm not going to sit here and tell you that money isn't important. Money is a driving force in our lives. But once you have the true necessities covered money stops being about the things you need and instead helps you buy the things you want. I could go on and on about the kind of trap that can create in your life. How the ever-turning wheel of needing more money to buy crap that you don't need to impress people you don't care about is keeping you trapped. Yes, I just invoked a Fight Club saying.

So, what happens when we are young and making professional decisions is that we see them as nearly permanent. We turn the decision into some endgame thought process. Which couldn't be further from the truth. A study of baby boomers showed that the average number of jobs held in a lifetime came out to eleven. Folks, let me repeat that statistic. That was baby boomers, not millennials, who are more transient with their careers according to another study performed by Gallup.

To top it all off we make that decision based on terrible information and inputs. If your father hated his job and made it known throughout the household what do you think the chances are that you would want a job like his? Pretty low, right? But you aren't your father. The things that make you tick may not be things that made your father tick. Maybe you are money motivated but your older brother was motivated by a desire to make a difference through his profession. By the way, if you are money motivated that is ok. Just admit it to yourself and keep that in mind as you decide whether you are better suited as an employee or an entrepreneur.

The reality is that your career choices are not as big a decision as you are making them out to be. A career is an infinitely more fluid thing than that. My career is a perfect example. In my twenty-plus years as a professional, I have been a martial arts instructor, a salesperson, a marketer, a financial advisor, a bank teller, a researcher, and more. Those roles were across multiple industries. They weren't all within the financial sector.

The idea of bouncing around throughout your career may not excite you. Or, it might sound energizing to try so many different things. The point is that your career choices aren't an either/or kind of decision. There is a rearview mirror that you can look into and decide if you want to back up the car after taking the wrong road.

Higher Education's Role in Careers

The pressure to define who you want to be when you grow up only intensifies as you get closer to going to college. The most popular question asked for college seniors is about what college they will attend. The next most popular question is what their major will be.

The push to define your career path picks up steam as you get closer and closer to graduation. By the time you are a senior, you had better know what degree you are hoping to graduate with. Because the required coursework that goes with that degree is very specific. Changing your major as a freshman is not that big of a deal. It is pretty common. But as you progress in your collegiate world-changing majors becomes a big deal. Especially if you make a drastic change in majors. For example, changing from a business-based major to one that is science-based means that you will have all kinds of unfilled coursework that you need to back up and take.

As a freshman, I was a Management major. But by my sophomore year, I had switched to Marketing. Thank goodness they had a decent amount of overlap in the required coursework. Plus it was early enough in my college life that I had not got into the higher-level, major-specific courses. But I know plenty of people who did switch to areas of focus that they had to take years worth of new required classes.

Which is one of many reasons why I believe the education system in the United States is broken. The concept of picking a major area of focus during college makes sense on the surface. By doing so students focus their energy on becoming well-versed on a topic and therefore are supposedly better equipped to add value to a company when they graduate.

I contend that being so topically focused truly limits people's career choices. Sure, you can use a Marketing degree at just about any company. You can also leverage what you learned about Marketing as an entrepreneur. You need to understand Marketing as an entrepreneur.

The truth is that whether your career choices lead you done the road of climbing the corporate ladder or experiencing the entrepreneurial grind that you are going to need a lot more about a wide variety of topics or majors. Entrepreneurs aren't the only professionals that end up having to be the bookkeeper, marketer, salesperson, manager, finance officer, and janitor. As employees, your early career may be compartmentalized to your area of focus during college. But more than likely the higher up the corporate ladder you climb the more you are going to need to know about all of those topics and the one class you took on organizational behavior isn't going to be enough.

That is why I don't see college as a place to help you determine your career path. You simply aren't exposed to enough choices and don't get a chance to understand what those career choices will mean to you. Plus, if you do decide to change paths in the middle of your college experience you are almost penalized by having to pick another path. There just isn't enough flexibility in that type of setup.

Where college does shine is that it is a great place to be exposed to how other students are thinking about their careers. In college, you are going to come across all kinds of different people. Each one of them will be thinking about their future differently.

Some of them won't share the same motivations as you have. Others will share your motivations. The second group is the one I want you to find and spend time around. By spending time around people with similar motivations as you there is a better chance that you will make smarter career choices. Conversely, hanging around other students who don't share your motivations is a bad idea.

If you are focused on making a difference with your career and your pal Chris is very money motivated and views his career strictly as a way to create personal wealth then you shouldn't be hanging around him for professional guidance.

False Advertising

One of the biggest challenges around choosing a career path is the lack of transparency from other professionals. At least, that is my take on things.

Rarely do you see professionals being utterly transparent about how they feel about their own career choices.

There are no better examples than all of the online entrepreneurs that are running around advertising on Facebook and other social media channels offering to teach you how to make a living, or even a fortune, through passive income channels.

Now, I know this is already coming off as a rant. I'm not saying that passive income isn't possible. Because I have multiple streams of passive income coming into my bank account. But, they took a long time to build and in some instances they took a significant investment from me or my family.

Entrepreneurs aren't the only professionals that are falsely advertising. Corporate professionals are sugar-coating their experiences as well. Think about it. If you have ever asked pointed questions during a job interview when is the last time someone was willing to admit that the company was difficult to work for. Even if they are honest with you about how things are they tend to quickly auto-correct and refocus on how things are "getting better".

Occasionally you will get the truth from someone. Today I experienced such honesty.

For almost two years now I have been a member of an online community. The business owner is a brilliant marketer. He, and most of the other community members, live in the United Kingdom. Not only have I learned a massive amount about marketing from him and the other members but I have also come to call many of them my close friends. Even though I have never met a single member in person.

So, when he announced that the business was closing I was

stunned. Not just because I felt I would be losing a direct link to that community, but also because he was willing to be utterly open about why he was shuttering the business.

The fact was that the business was not supporting itself and that he did not see that changing in the near future. The owner and the rest of the team had spent the last year investing in the business with the belief that things would turn profitable in the future.

That kind of story isn't one that you read about online very often. But it is the reality.

The Millennial Effect

A few generations ago, I am in Generation X, it was very common for professionals to work for one company for their entire career. It was seen as a smart choice. Professionals stayed with their company for 40 years and then retired with a gold watch or some other item as their retirement gift.

However, in the past few decades, entrepreneurship has become more and more popular. As I have stated before, some part of that can be attributed to how the media tends to popularize being your own boss. You can also attribute a fair portion of the increase in entrepreneurial popularity toward the fact that the United States, for the most part, has had largely positive economic conditions for some time now. Another factor is that starting a business has never been easier. New technologies have enabled just about anyone interested to open a business much more quickly and for less money. All of that creates an ecosystem where starting a business is a bit less burdensome.

That is the kind of business atmosphere that the Millennial generation has grown up in. For people who experienced major economic events like the Great Depression, the World Wars, or even the Great Recession having to experience job loss impacted their career choices. Many turned toward entrepreneurship to control their fate. In fact,

While Millennials were alive during the Great Recession, but many of them weren't established as a professional just yet. So, some didn't experience job loss or the dramatic loss in the value of their retirement accounts.

Yet the Millennial generation as a whole, and the generation (Generation Z) after the Millennials, is one of the most entrepreneurial generations ever.
So, what is driving that phenomenon?

I mentioned above that new technologies are enabling more and more people to become business owners. For example, in today's business world having an online presence is a most. In the past creating a website took some level of technical skill. Today all you need is the ability to click a few buttons and you can have a website up and running in a matter of minutes through sites like Wix.com.

If you have a little bit more technology savvy you can host and build your own custom Wordpress site. I consider myself a beginner at Wordpress development. Yet, I've managed to build my website for every single business venture I have started.

If you want to run an online eCommerce site you can use existing technology like Shopify to list your products. Or, you can leverage Amazon's fulfillment centers to operate a dropshipping business. All without ever taking physical control of your inventory.

Some might argue that you don't even need a website in today's market. There are plenty of online business owners who are using just their phones and social media accounts to make a living.

While entrepreneurship is attractive to Millennials, with a recent survey finding that 58% of that generation considering themselves an entrepreneur, there is a segment of Millennials that are sticking to being an employee.

In 2018 Ladders.com released an article titled, "Survey: 86% of Millennials say they'd prefer to stay and grow within their company". Additional findings in that article showed that 56% of Millennials think people should stay with the same company "for more than 20 years". If your jaw didn't just fall open then allow me to be shocked for you. I don't know about you, but I have looked at plenty of resumes from that generation and those resumes don't show a pattern of staying at one company. But that is because of a legitimate reason. Millennials appear to value things like a flexible schedule and the ability to work on projects they are passionate about working on as much as, or possibly more than, the income they earn. When they aren't getting those things they move on to another company.

This could be why so many Millennials start their own side business. They want the security of working for someone else yet they want to express their creative side and work on projects that fulfill them in ways that their day job doesn't allow. A split professional life of having a day job and being a freelancer also allows them to control something else. They can control the number of hours they work.

I once hired a graphic designer named Nikki to help more come up with a logo for a new venture. Nikki fits into the Millennial generation and exactly matches my description above. She has a day job but also freelances at night. During a message conversation one day she explained to me that she liked having the security of the day job but freelanced to make extra money, when she needed it, and to work on projects that interested her.

When I asked whey Nikki had never decided to become a full-time entrepreneur she said that she did not want to have to "hustle all the time".

So, while there are some Millennials that yearn to be work for themselves there are also plenty that appears to enjoy working for someone else. Just under the right conditions.

What Do You Do?

What we do defines us. But it shouldn't.

I was "Mr. Networking" in my town for about seven years. During that time it wasn't uncommon for me to attend an event and already know about seventy-five percent of the attendees. Networking is one of those skills that I credit with why my career reached the point it did, how I survived multiple layoffs, and more.

There is no debate in my mind that networking is a skill that every professional, whether an employee or entrepreneur, must have.

To me, there is an art form in networking well. Some professionals are terrible at it. Some even hate it. I don't blame them. They probably hate networking because they met people who were terrible at it. Those professionals that are terrible at it tend to see networking as a contact sport as a collector. Meaning that they only focus on the initial contact with other professionals and collect their business cards.

These are the same people whose first question when they meet someone new is "What do you do?". Whip out the measuring stick, folks. Because you have just been weighed and found either worthy or not worthy.

I despise that question. Because even people that ask it in good faith are still using it to measure you against themselves. That or they are trying to figure out if there is something you can do for them professionally.

Men are particularly bad at using this question to size each other up. It is like some proverbial pissing contest where they measure whose d.....who makes the most money.

We could easily attribute this one question as part of the career struggle that people go through in their lives. I can't speak for you ladies, but I know that most men are largely defined by what they do for a living. We don't carry around little pieces of paper that say that we are a dad, husband, and gaming enthusiast. We carry around business cards that say which company we work for or own, what our title is, and how to get in touch with us.

Just look at the answers I received on the survey I prepared in my research on this whole topic. When I asked people to tell me about themselves, respondents from both genders couldn't help it and used their titles or profession. The very first person to answer the survey used one word, entrepreneur, when asked to describe themselves. Think about that answer. This individual is so defined by the fact that they have started their own business that they felt that is all they needed to share. There was nothing about his family, education, or hobbies. It was the thing that takes up between eight to twenty hours of their daily lives that described them. The other answers were just as eye-opening. One respondent even went so far as to mention that he had gone through two careers in his life.

Interestingly, only one survey respondent listed their personal life before their professional career. When asked to describe herself, Anita Lane started with the fact that she is a wife and a mother. Whereas most respondents went straight to defining themselves by their professional title or career, Anita identifies herself first by her choice to have a family. Yet, in terms of career success, she is just as successful, if not more so, than the vast majority of people that I interviewed for this book.

Those answers got me thinking about a great question I have heard used in the past with people who are struggling with their career choices. That question is, "if money were not an issue what would you do with your life?". That is the wrong question to ask. Because money is always going to matter. The days of the barter system are long gone. Instead, ask how much money you need.

My First Exposure to Entrepreneurship

I grew up idolizing my father. Not only was he a fantastic father, but he was also a very successful business professional.

As a kid, we moved around the United States a fair amount. I was originally born in Atlanta, Georgia. By the time I was a freshman in high school we had lived in Georgia, North Carolina, back to Georgia, California, Florida, and South Carolina.

When people learn about all the moves we experienced they usually want to know if we were a military family. While my father did serve in the National Guard, his career was actually in the logistics and transportation industry.

We moved so much because my father was very, very good at his job. By his early thirties, he was running the largest distribution center for a national fast-food chain. From there he was promoted to Vice President and told that his paycheck was in California. No sooner had we settled down there than he was promoted to Senior Vice President and told to relocate to Southern Florida. At that time my older brother had a few years of high school to finish. So, my parents decided to let him graduate before we moved to Florida. Thus began about a two-year stint of my father living near Miami and commuting back to Northern California about every two weeks.

I have very distinct memories of my father's corporate career. Even at a young age, I could tell that people, whether supervisors or people that worked for him, really respected and trusted him. My brother and I use to visit him at the facility in Atlanta where he was the General Manager. He always had a very easy-going manner about the way he interacted with people in professional settings. But, he could also be very intense when he needed to be. The ability to balance those two personalities most likely played a huge role in his career advancement.

Eventually, his run in the corporate world came to an abrupt end. In 1988, following a fallout with leadership, my father decided to try his hand at entrepreneurship. He had dabbled at it a few different times, but it had never stuck.

However, this time would be different.

Over the next few years, he would launch and grow, with my older brother's help, a logistics and purchasing consulting business that would go from $3 million to $75 million under management. As well as becoming a partner in a 10+ unit restaurant chain.

Unfortunately, my father passed away in 2016. So, I never got the opportunity to dig deeper into his choice to become an entrepreneur. I suspect, after the 1988 fallout with his company, he could have easily found another corporate job. Instead, he took the gamble and launched a business that even today is providing for our family.

I do know enough, from piecing together our conversations and talking with my mother, to know that he had become disenchanted with the office politics that were associated with his high-level position. One of his favorite sayings was, "The higher up you are the closer you are to the door". The stress from his high-level position and the associated responsibilities had also taken a toll on his health in the form of colitis. I suspect the combination of all of those factors plus the years of moving had pushed him to the point of no return.

As I grow older I've thought a lot about what it must have taken for my father to leap into self-employment. There had to be so much to factor into that decision. I've even wondered just how close he got in the end to going back to work for other people. Or, if because he was able to make enough of money in the early days if he just decided to stick with it.

It's not like starting a business wasn't a huge roll of the dice. At least in many ways.

If you look at the experience and skills he had to fall back on you might think it was a "no brainer" decision. After all, he was making the company he was working for a fortune. Surely it was safe to assume he could do that for his new clients and therefore himself. But entrepreneurship isn't that easy.

When my father's career change occurred he was at the

height of his corporate career. With that came all kinds of benefits that a lot of corporate professionals dream of. He was making an extremely healthy income, he had a prestigious title, he worked for a well-known and respected company, and he had peers that he called friends and who respected him. Not to mention a sizeable retirement package that included a pension.

All of that would have been so easy to go back to after he had been able to catch his breath. Plus, he had a lot of responsibilities pulling on him. After all, he was the family breadwinner. He had a wife and two kids to provide for and a few financial responsibilities. One of which was a pretty hefty house payment.

Sure, my parents had some money set aside in savings. But over the next few years, they would churn through a decent amount of that while Dad's company got up and running.

Yet, with all of that factored into his decision he decided to go for it. As far as I could tell he never, I mean never, looked back.

Looking back now I know that isn't true. There is a reason that whenever I would stop in to visit him that he was always grinding away at one thing or another in his business. I imagine that is because, no matter how much I thought my father was Superman, he was always worried that it all would come crashing down. So, even though I never directly asked him whether he had deliberately chosen to stay an entrepreneur and if he ever thought about giving it up, I know without a doubt that he had huge reservations. I just suspect those reservations weren't as scary or as stressful as he saw the alternative being.

While the early years as an entrepreneur were very difficult they eventually turned around for my father.

Early on he had to piece together a living by taking on contract work that supplemented the consulting he was doing. But somewhere around the late 90s, I remember the company hitting a stride. He had survived long enough to establish himself.

That was right about the time he decided to expand by bringing my older brother into the company. He followed up that by "retiring" my mother. Now, she will tell you that she did the furthest thing from retiring. I know without a doubt that she put just as many hours into the business as she had her career.

Between the three of them, they managed to turn the company into a true enterprise. From there they each expanded into other business ventures. My brother started a mortgage company and my parents became partners in a local restaurant chain.

As with most businesses things weren't always rosy. For example, I remember the company losing one of its top clients, and therefore the associated revenue, just about the time my brother had decided to move into a bigger house. There was also a failed attempt at opening a new restaurant location that also set the business back.

Still, my father weathered it all. What he pulled off, as he was nearing the end of his battle with cancer, was nothing short of an amazing business accomplishment.

Looking back, I would have told you that I didn't see my father as an entrepreneur. He was risk-averse and made plenty of decisions out of fear. But the truth is that the title just didn't suit him. Because he was just doing what it took to provide for his family.

There is a line in one of the Iron Man movies where Tony Stark discovers the hidden design his father made of the first Arc Reactor. The line is, "Still schooling me after all these years". As an entrepreneur, my father is still schooling me to this day. The same is true as a husband and father.

My Own Entrepreneurial Ventures

Over the years I have interviewed hundreds of entrepreneurs. Many as part of the SouthFound startup podcast series that I hosted for six seasons. It probably will come as no surprise to you that the vast majority of those founders were exposed to entrepreneurship by someone in their family.

My entrepreneurial journey was influenced by my father's ventures. I suppose I should also give some credit to my maternal grandfather who ran a successful jewelry business until his retirement in the 80s. There is little doubt in my mind that seeing the success that both of those men experienced is part of the reason that I have always wanted to own my own business.

But, my path to entrepreneurship has always had a much more gray startling line. While my father and grandfather both leaped into the pool with both feet, I have always kept one foot in the corporate world. However, there are some similarities between how my father got started and how I became interested in creating businesses.

Before I talk about my business ventures I should take a moment to share my corporate experience.

I graduated from college with a degree in Marketing. My focus in school was largely around market research. After graduation, I didn't go straight to work in a corporate setting. Instead, I continued as the head instructor at a martial arts school that I had worked at off and on through college. I had chosen to stay in that role because I was competing full-time and was in first place in my state. In 1996 I finished the season as the Tennessee State Grand Champion. Having accomplished that personal goal I decided it was time to move on and put my education to work.

So, I took a job as a Marketing Coordinator for a water purification company. I was so excited to be able to put to use al the things I had learned in college. Unfortunately, I would end up spending more time doing phone and in-person sales than the type of marketing work I was hoping to do.

From there I joined the family restaurant business as a manager. To everyone that works in that industry, I salute you. Because it can be a very tough business. Particularly in dealing with the public via serving people food and the long hours you often end up working. After almost three years of working seventy-two hours a week and only having one day off a week, I decided it was time to move on.

Luckily my sister-in-law was able to help me get a job selling insurance over the phone. I didn't enjoy that job either. So, while going through some personal relationship changes I decided it was time to do something drastic about my professional life.

In 2001 I moved to Japan. I had originally signed on to teach English under a one-year contract. That lasted all of six weeks. The experience ended up being nothing like I thought it was going to be. I assumed I would be able to immerse myself in Japan and thereby learn the language and culture. My plan was to live boldly through this experience while learning a second language that I could then leverage in the business world. Instead, I learned that, at least in my personal experience, the Japanese didn't want to speak their language with a gaijin (a foreigner). They wanted to practice their English.

There was another problem with my move overseas. Two months before I was scheduled to leave I started dating my wife. Having been through a bad prior relationship I was determined to not allow a woman to hold me back. To her credit, she did the right thing in encouraging me to continue with my plan to move to Japan.

But once I got there and realized that the experience wasn't going to be what I had hoped I quickly decided that it was time to return home. I was away from my family and now I had this amazing person that I wanted to spend my life with. I'll never forget calling my dad from a Kyoto phone booth and asking him if I could charge a flight home to his credit card. The next day I slept in the Osaka airport while I waited on standby for a flight home.

The started a period of my professional life where I took

the time to explore my career options. Which included a stint as a financial advisor and getting my real estate license but never pursuing the business. I was starting to like the idea of working in the financial sector but I wasn't sure which part of that world I belonged in. Until a co-worker suggested I look into banking.

Around 2002 I started my career in banking. That path would take me from a teller, to head teller, to branch manager, then working as a small business lender, to a commercial lender, and finally as a Chief Lending Officer.

The thing is, I never really planned to be a banker. I just knew that I liked working with numbers and finances. This is why I will talk more in this book about why you shouldn't focus on industries or titles and focus more on your skill set and where you can apply those skills. Regardless of whether or not you choose to be an employee or an entrepreneur.

It is because of the skills I learned in my corporate life and the skills I taught my self by staying up late at night that have allowed me to do the things I now do professionally. That includes starting and running my businesses.

My first business venture goes back to being in 8th grade in Florida. Back then I was obsessed with collectible cards, particularly baseball cards. Around that time a new line of baseball cards came into the market. Originally Topps and Donruss were the top brands. But when Score entered the space I was an early adopter of their cards. That is how I found my first business opportunity.

Because I was such a fan of the Score brand of cards I was convinced that other kids would be as well. Since they were so new it was really hard to get your hands on their cards. Luckily, I never experienced that problem. So, my first business was buying boxes of Score baseball cards and reselling the individual packs to other kids at school. Unfortunately, I didn't make a lot of money. Mostly because I had a habit of consuming my own product. Still, I enjoyed the process of running a business and selling a product. Plus, I learned a lot along the way about marketing, accounting, etc.

Even though I enjoyed running my baseball card business

it would be years before I decided to try my hand at starting up another venture.

After graduating college I was convinced that I wanted to climb the corporate ladder and be a CEO one day. Which would eventually become a possibility (more on that later). In a bit of a roundabout way, I ended up in the finance industry where my corporate career began to accelerate. In about seven years I went from being a bank teller to being the Chief Lending Officer at a $230 million financial institution. During those seven years, I spent a lot of time around entrepreneurs as a Commercial Loan Officer. Because I was so well-connected in my community I became "the guy" to call when you needed funding for a business. Which is how I got involved in the startup world.

Over my career, I have been involved in well over half a billion dollars (that's $500,000,000) in funding for businesses. A large part of that is debt financing via commercial loans, but I have also helped entrepreneurs raise millions of dollars from investors.

Most of the banks that I worked for at the time would never have considered making a loan to a startup. But that did not stop them from approaching me and the various banks I worked at for funding. After a while, I got tired of telling each startup founder that I could not help them. So, I decided to learn about and get involved in venture capital.

Being around the startup industry taught me one thing. That is that if you are experiencing a pain point with someone in your life and you have a unique solution for easing that pain point then you most likely have a good idea for a business. After years and years of networking, I definitely had a pain point. I was tired of talking to the same people at networking events and wanted to meet people that I did not know but should know. That is how GoGrabLunch was created.

In 2010, I created and launched a first-of-its-kind business-to-business networking site where like-minded professionals could connect over coffee or lunch to help grow each other's business by developing deep referral relationships. The model allowed professionals to set up a profile and tell our system the types of professionals that they would benefit from getting to know. Our system then matched those professionals, allowed them to go grab lunch together and get to know one another. It was kind of like modern dating sights but for professional purposes. We even built-in control to keep out the personal dating aspect.

As my first serious venture, the business did pretty well. By the time I closed the business we had members in 45 countries and had been pursued by various venture capital firms as well as were being pursued by one of the top social media networks for a possible joint venture. You can read more about the whole experience jonathanmillspatrick.com/ebooks/.

I closed that business for a variety of reasons. One of which was that my corporate career was taking off. I was also winning national recognition for another startup idea that I had created and launched while at the financial institution where I was Chief Lending Officer. Plus, I was being told that I could one day succeed the CEO when she retired.

While I couldn't see stepping away from the potential benefits that brought, the entrepreneurial spirit never fully went away. That is why even today I am working in a corporate role but also continue to run my own business as a consultant to companies ranging from true startups to my largest client who is a Fortune 30 tech giant.

So, why am I sharing all of this with you? What do my family's professional background and my own professional experience have to do with helping you make your own choices about whether you would be better off professional as an employee or as an entrepreneur?

Because along the way you are going to hear from a lot of other professionals who have been in your shoes. Some have been employees with amazing corporate careers but they have chosen to leave that life and start their own business. Some have been entrepreneurs and have decided that such a life is not right for them for a variety of reasons.

I hope that the experiences they share along the way, including my insights, will provide you with all of the information you need to decide if your path is better suited for the ladder or the grind.

Factors in Career Choices

In this section, I will lay out some of the key factors that I think you should consider when trying to make a career choice. These factors are important when you are trying to decide between two jobs as an employee. But they are also just as important when deciding between climbing the corporate ladder or grinding away as an entrepreneur.

You may not agree with my perspective on these factors. Or, you might have other factors you think that I missed. That isn't the point. The key is that you at least consider the various factors that would impact a career decision for you.

It is especially important that you also consider the order of those factors. Meaning that you consider which factors are the most important to you.

Many of these factors were included in the survey I asked people to complete. As you might see, the order of priority of those factors for the majority of people that answered the survey could surprise you. I know it surprised me.

The point of the survey was to see if there was a pattern behind the types of factors that motivated professionals to choose the path of an employee or the path toward entrepreneurship.

I first asked respondents to choose which single factor was the main driving force behind their career choices. They could choose money, flexibility in their schedule, the ability to express themselves creatively, a professional title, or recognition. There was also the option to fill in their answer which a few people did.

Next, I asked respondents which of those same factors would be their second-highest priority in choosing a career path. Some of the factors I will be discussing didn't make it onto the survey. But they did show up in the interviews I conducted. Regardless of how each factor was uncovered the truth is that two or three of the factors dominated the findings.

Try not to cheat and look ahead. Without doing that can you guess which of the factors was the most common factor in people's career choices?

Let me help you out with the choices I gave people. They were money, flexibility in their schedule, the ability to express themselves creatively, a professional title, recognition, or other. I'll give you two hints. It was one of the options I gave people, not the "Other" choice. Also, it probably isn't the factor you think it is.

Now, I know that a survey and its findings are only so good as the respondents that take the survey. I did my best to get a nice cross-sample of professionals to take the survey. Frankly, I would have liked to have had more answers. But, I still believe that the information I uncovered is really valuable.

As you read through each of the factors and my thoughts on those factors, be sure to think about how you feel about each factor. Is that factor one that ranks high in priority for you and your career choices? Is it the most important factor? Or, maybe two factors rank equally high. It could even be that one factor is more important to you right now based on your current professional environment.

Either way, use this section to help you hone in on what matters to you. Because once you know the answer to that only then can we begin to dial-in your choices to get you closer to the type of career that will help you feel the most fulfilled. Be that the ladder or the grind.

Express Yourself

When it comes to career choices, it would seem that money is a backdrop to one other motivating factor. At least that is true of the people that took the research survey for this book.

You might recall that in the money section of this book I shared that money was the second most important factor. It wasn't even close. Of the people that participated in the survey, money was almost three times more likely to impact people's choices over flexibility in their schedule (25%) and recognition (12.5%).

There are a couple of interesting findings in there.

First, the sheer fact that money got second place. Second, that more respondents valued money over having flexibility in their schedule. I'll talk about that in the section on flexibility.

So, if money played second fiddle to another factor what was the main thing that motivated people's career choices?

The ability to express one's self creatively was three times more likely to be the key factor in the type of career that people pursued.

That means that using one's creativity was the equivalent of three times more important to professionals than what they could earn, six times more important than flexibility, and twelve times more important than recognition.

Security, which is super important to me, barely even made the list. As did other factors.

When I initially saw that expressing one's self ranked so highly I immediately assumed that factor was winning out because people were feeling the draw to work on things that they were passionate about. Because by digging further I couldn't equate that data point with the industries that the respondents worked in. Meaning, that there weren't a bunch of artists answering the survey that was skewing the results. But, that just wasn't the case.

Nor was it a matter of having more full-time entrepreneurs than corporate professionals answer the survey. On that point twenty-five percent of respondents were entrepreneurs and the remaining were climbing the corporate ladder.

But, interestingly, it was the entrepreneurs that drove home the need for expressing themselves. Because for every entrepreneur that was their primary motivating factor. Whereas the answer from the corporate respondents was thinly spread out across all other factors.

What I am saying is that the entrepreneurs unequivocally wanted to have careers where they could be creative. That probably isn't a huge shock to you. But it kind of was one to me. Because I had assumed that flexibility and our money would be the first pick of the entrepreneurs. Those weren't even the second pick for that group.

I also had assumed that at least a few of the corporate folks would have answered that they wanted to have a career where they could express themselves. But that didn't hold true either. The whole reason that money was the second choice was exactly because of the day-job group.

Let me try to bring this point full-circle for you.

Based on the survey entrepreneurs focus their career choices on paths that allow them to be themselves. Work that allows them to express who they are is the most important thing to them. Not money. Not recognition. And not a title. You might say that they just want fulfillment in what they do.

In contrast, people who work for someone else appear to value money, by a huge gap, over any other motivating factor. The best part is those that I spoke to about this point were unabashedly money motivated. They didn't want to express themselves. They wanted to get paid.

All of this leads me to another leap in thinking. Were the entrepreneurs saying that money wasn't important because they were already making a very good living? Not in the least. Nearly all of the entrepreneurs that answered the survey were either losing money in their venture(s) or were merely making a meager living. Most were making less money than many of the corporate people.

But, they had something the corporates did not have.

They were being fulfilled by working on something that matters to them. By being able to express their true colors and to be who they knew they were.

Money

It isn't uncommon to meet an employee who feels like they are underpaid. Did you know that in the first quarter of 2019 the average employee salary was over $47,000? If we just look at people with college degrees that number jumps up to over $70,000. Folks without a college degree averaged around $30,000 a year in income.

Here's the interesting part about those statistics. Regardless of your education, those numbers are more than the average amount of income needed, regardless of which US State you live in, to "get by".

Listen, I know that no one wants to just "get by". I get it. We all have a fundamental desire to grow and to have more. But the concept of having more is more about your wants. Not your needs. You want a new car. You don't need one if you already have one that can safely get you around town without too many problems. You want a nicer house with a three-car garage. But your cars won't implode if they have to sit out on the driveway. Yes, scraping ice off your windshield is an inconvenience. But, it is just that.

So, when you say you want to make more money the vast majority of people I have talked to are saying that they want more discretionary spending power. They will talk a big game about saving more or putting more into their retirement accounts. But that rarely happens.

Most of the people that I have coached on the topic of finances tend to increase the amount of money they spend in step with the amount of extra income they just earned.

I know I've done that in the years gone by. Every time I got a raise or a fat bonus check it went to some expense that was usually new. Get a raise? Buy a new house. Earn a bonus? Buy a boat. And I am not alone. How do I know that to be the case? Just look at where people spend their money. They want to have the nicer things in life.

However important you view money as being in your life,

you might be surprised to learn that it wasn't the primary factor in the people's career choices that I interviewed. But, it was the second most important factor. That point didn't change regardless of whether they were working for themselves or working for someone else. Money played a huge role in their professional choices.

Does that shock you at all? Not the part about money as the second most important factor. I'm asking if it shocks you that money was the second most important factor in career choices whether the person interviewed was an employee or an entrepreneur. It shocked me for sure. The reason was that I was under the impression that people choose to be entrepreneurs because they are very, very money motivated. After all, entrepreneurs do make more money than employees, right? Surely you are under the same impression that I am. I mean, I thought I knew what you are thinking about here. "But Jonathan, entrepreneurs make more money than employees!". Not so fast. We are going to look at that and I can assure you that you will be surprised by the numbers.

Income research firm Payscale published in February 2019 that the income range for a small business owner was between $30,000 and $182,000, with the average being around $72,000. According to their research, via the Bureau of Labor Statistics, the average employee made just over $56,000. So, while the average entrepreneur did make a bit more than the average employee the difference is not substantial. Plus, there is a piece of the puzzle that those numbers don't address. Entrepreneurs have to pay for their benefits and more. So, is that $70,000 average gross or net? Either way, you need to ask yourself if an extra $16,000 is worth the stress of running your own business. It might be worth it to you. Or, you might decide that an extra $1,000 per month, after taxes, just doesn't cut it.

Security

What is the biggest asset that most people have? Lots of people would tell you that it is your home. That people believe that makes sense with median house prices running about $200,000. But your home isn't your biggest asset. It isn't an investment either. Because you can likely earn a higher rate of return through other investment vehicles. But, more on that some other time.

Your biggest asset is your income potential. Plain and simple, whether you are an employee or an entrepreneur, the asset that you need to protect the most is your paycheck. Take that away and most people will almost immediately be in financial distress. Especially since the average household can't afford a $400 emergency.

That is why job security, or we could call it income security to include entrepreneurs, is such a key factor in many people's choice of a career path. That is also why job security continues to rank very high in importance to people who work for someone else.

Income security is one of the reasons that I have never completely shifted from being an employee to being an entrepreneur. It is also one of the reasons that I continue to have "Plan B" businesses running at all times. Meaning a business that is generating income in case I lose the ability to make a living through my primary source of income. That way if something happens to my day job I can try to quickly ramp up income from my side hustles.

At least when you work for someone else, particularly a large company, there is a very high chance that you can count on your paycheck not bouncing. Now, I will say that I have worked for companies before where the employees wondered if their paychecks would bounce or not. One of those companies was my first "real job" in Marketing. I worked for a water purification startup that was being funded by a wealthy individual. At one point he got so tired of a lack of progress that he threatened to let the company fold and to stop funding the payroll account.

Whereas, when you are an entrepreneur your income security is only as good as your ability to sell your products and services or "eat what you kill". Which is scary for some people. For others, they love that idea because they recognize that it means they don't have a limit on their income potential. Which also means that their income can be zero some times.

If what I just said is true, then working for someone else is the much safer choice when it comes to income security, right? Not so fast. As an entrepreneur, you might lose clients and the revenue associated with that client. You burn through cash trying to attract new clients through your advertising or marketing efforts. But you can't lose your job. If a company fires you or lays you off from your job there is nothing you can do about getting that income back immediately. But if you are an entrepreneur and your last client leaves you there is still the option of landing a new client. That might be tougher than it sounds. But at least that is an option.

While as an employee you can reasonably be assured that your paycheck will be good you can't count on having that paycheck because you can be laid off or fired at any time. I've personally been laid off three times. The last time it happened I was a top-performer at my company. So, if you are thinking that your income is secure because you kick ass at your job you had better think again.

The reality is that, regardless of whether you choose the ladder or the grind, there is no such thing as income security. Ever. I know that it can be hard to admit to that to yourself. I know that is really, really scary. But it is very freeing once you realize that the idea of income security is a myth. The good news is that in most instances when you lose a job or your business runs out of cash the results aren't fatal. No one in my household died when I got laid off.

It got a little scary for sure. Especially seeing our bank account balance drop. But, we made it work until I found another job. I'll admit that it felt pretty catastrophic the time I was laid off and our daughter was nine months old. I can distinctly remember wondering how I was going to put food on the table. We had some savings set aside, but not enough to survive on for more than a few months.

I can tell you without a moment's hesitation that those memories are why I continue to hustle so much professionally. Because I was determined to never be in that position again. While we are in an infinitely better financial position now I can still look in the mirror and admit that job security doesn't exist. But there are things that you can do to reduce your chances of losing your income security.

For example, as an employee, some industries are much more prone to layoffs than others. According to statistics from the Bureau of Labor Statistics layoffs across the United States have been running at about 1.2% from June 2018 until June 2019. Industries that saw higher layoff averages than the national average included construction (2.6%), professional services (2%), and entertainment (as high as 4.8%!). The industries that appear to provide some level of safety from layoffs included manufacturing, wholesale trade, financial, real estate, health care, and government. Each of those industries averaged less than a 1% layoff rate. The government sector had the lowest layoff rate. There are even regions of the United States that statistically see higher levels of layoffs. For example, the same report from the Bureau of Labor Statistics showed that the South (where I live, yippy!) had higher levels of layoffs than any other region. The rest of the US Say relatively comparable levels of layoffs.

Security in your professional doesn't just come down to whether or not your industry is susceptible to layoffs. At least not in my opinion. Some parts of security could also be attributed to how long people tend to stay in a given industry or profession. That is otherwise known as tenure.

I include tenure in the security discussion because the longer a person stays in their profession signals to me a few possible things. They could be content with what they do for a living and/or they could feel secure in their industry and job.

Of course, a long tenure could come down to the fact that the person was trained specifically for that profession and they don't feel like they can change jobs. But the reality is that they could change professions at any time. That happens all the time. Websites like Career Advice Online claim that 30% of employees change careers every 12 months. They even go so far as to say that employers now expect to see resumes with a lot of career changes.

If you take a look at which industries have a tenure ratio that is higher than the average, the average in 2018 being 3.8 years for private-sector employees according to the Bureau of Labor, you start to see a trend. The industries with high tenure ratios do, in fact, also have lower than average layoff ratios. For example, according to Business Insider, almost every manufacturing sector say tenure ratios over 5 years.

Those are all private sector tenure statistics. If you take into account the tenure ratios that public sector employees carry the correlation between layoffs, or a lack thereof, and tenure gets even stronger. I mentioned above that government workers saw the lowest layoff rate in all industries. They also appear to have one of the longest tenures, almost 10 years worth, of all industries. A lack of layoffs adds to that length of tenure. But, there has to be more to it, right?

I'm not suggesting that job security isn't a huge perk for government employees. Even if you have never worked in a government role I think we could all agree that job security appears to be one of the top perks that those workers experience. Without even looking at the statistics we could all probably assume that those employees aren't staying for the income potential that they experience. The fact that the private sector tends to pay more than the public sector seems to be widely known.

Of course, being in an industry that has a low layoff ratio or having a long tenure with your company doesn't entirely shelter you either. Particularly in periods of an economic downturn like a recession. I found that out to be true.

In 2007 I left my job as a commercial lender for a super-regional bank. Ever since joining the banking industry my career track had quickly progressed. In a few short years I went from being a teller to a head teller, to an assistant branch manager, to a small business lender, and finally landing a role as a commercial lender.

That kind of role was one I had wanted ever since joining the industry. I saw the commercial lender role as a very prestigious role. From my days as a teller, I had watched as my institutions' commercial lenders were treated as if they were the rockstars of the bank. They got to land big deals that came with big bonus checks all while playing golf and networking with prospects and clients. They weren't trapped in an office and experienced the kind of flexibility I wanted.

So, when I was promoted to a commercial lending role I was so excited. I felt as is I had finally arrived in at my dream job. For the longest time, it was just that. I had a great run and eventually ended up doing over $500,000,000 (that's half a billion dollars) in business over my time as a commercial lender. Eventually, the role lost its luster. I grew tired of having to reset the clock on the amount of production I needed to do every year. Plus, I had a boss who liked to treat her employees like they were her five-year-old. As the saying goes, people don't quit jobs they quit managers. So, I decided to take a position in a slightly different position in the finance industry.

That experiment lasted about a year until I experienced my second layoff. The newspaper where I was serving as the credit manager went through a reorganization and decided to outsource a lot of their accounting functions to India. I discovered the details of that move when I found a packet on the public printer titled, "Outsourcing Your Accounting to India".

Leaving the parking lot that day I was able to immediately land two interviews by leveraging my network. Both were back in the banking industry as a commercial lender. I wasn't thrilled to be returning to the industry so quickly. But, it was the industry I knew the best and where most of my skills at the time could be helpful.

That experience lasted just over two years until I experienced my third layoff. I learned about that when I noticed on my bosses calendar that he had back-to-back meetings book with me, one other teammate, and the assistant we shared.

The thing is that I was one of the top producers on the team. So, was my teammate that got let go. If that was true, why were we the ones to be laid off instead of the other three team members who weren't producing as much? Because I know for a fact that the decision wasn't production-based. My boss said as much.

Instead, we got beat out by tenured employees. My teammate and I were the two newest hires in commercial lending. Two of three other team members had both been at the company for over twenty years.

When a company decides to do layoffs they most often pay a severance package to the employees being let go. Those packages vary, but in my experience, you can generally count on one-week of pay for every year you have been at the company. So, if you are the Chief Financial Officer looking at the impact of those severance packages would you rather pay someone twenty-plus weeks of severance or two weeks of severance?

Let me bring us full circle back to my earlier point. Some industries are safer than others. Banking was not a very industry to be in during the early days of the 2008-2009 financial crisis that is now called The Great Recession. So, I had that going against me.

But, I also didn't have the kind of tenure that many of my co-workers had. I was outperforming many of them. But it was too easy for my company to take all of my accounts and hand them over to someone else who would have been ten times more expensive to let go of in terms of a severance expense.

So, what am I saying? Again, I'm saying that the idea of complete and utter income security is a myth. Regardless of whether you work for yourself or someone else. But, some things can improve your chances of not losing your income. Like the industry you are in and your tenure in your position. As an employee, those two factors can create a nice protective shield that can create a nice layer of job security for you. As an entrepreneur, you can protect your stream of income by having a diverse portfolio of clients, by not over-extending yourself, and having plenty of money saved up for those months that run a bit dry.

Kids

My wife and I had our daughter when I was thirty-four years old. Between our time dating and being just a husband and wife, we had been together for seven years before we made the deliberate decision to become parents.

I call it a deliberate decision because that is what it truly was. I can vividly remember us having that conversation and making the decision to start trying to conceive. That memory is so alive to me because that was a decision that I didn't even think we would make as a couple. I had taught kids karate for years and enjoyed doing so. I enjoyed being "Uncle Joe". But I never thought about having my kids. My wife was very much of the same mindset in that she never thought she would have kids. Or get married for that matter. Turns out I am quite the salesman.

We had decided to start trying earlier but both backed off the idea. After returning from a trip to Costa Rica, around the middle of May of 2007, we decided to it was time.

Thank God we made that decision. Because I can tell you without a single bit of hesitation that being a father is the single best decision I have ever made and the thing that brings me the most joy in my life.

Why am I telling you all of this? Because I want you to understand before I talk about how kids can impact your career choices, that I see children as a complete and utter blessing.

Of the people that took the book's survey about one-third of them did not have children. The remaining majority, or two-thirds, did have kids. Over half of the respondents that did not have children were full-time entrepreneurs.

What I don't know is if they elected not to have children or if they biologically couldn't have children. Regardless, for full-time entrepreneurs, not having children played a huge factor in their career choice to have and run their own business.

Their rationale was similar to the thought process that we saw around marriage except that it was inverse. There we saw that being married added another factor to a person's career choices that had to be considered. That being another person's life was going to be impacted by their professional choices. The inverse was true for full-time entrepreneurs without children. They felt freer to choose to be an entrepreneur and accept the risks that came with that choice because they did not have "another mouth to feed".

So, again, what am I saying? I'm saying that, when it comes to making career choices, the more factors that have to be taken into consideration the less likely most professionals are to choose what they see as the riskier path. Professionals with others to think about, whether married and/or having kids, saw entrepreneurship as that risker path.

But, I don't want you to read this section and decide that because you have children or want to have them one day that you can't decide to work for yourself. On the contrary, I see having children as a reason you should pursue entrepreneurship.

What better motivation do you need to try and improve your family's future than little ones?

I know our daughter is a constant source of motivation and encouragement to me to try and make the right career choices. She is one of the reasons I sought out a job where I could work from home. I can be having a busy or tough day and taking a break to see and talk to her can help me reset mentally. In the summers there isn't much better than using my lunch break to play a board game and eat lunch together. She is also the reason I pursue side hustles. Beyond exploring my creativity and proving that I can grow a business I want to provide for my daughter and my wife so that we can enjoy our time together with amazing experiences.

So, let your kids be the reason you make certain career choices. But don't rush off and blindly take on more risk by working for an insolvent company or starting your own business without a financial safety net.

Flexibility

One of the reasons that people look negatively on being an employee is that they often feel that they don't have the kind of flexibility that they'd like. The 2018 Global Talent Trends report found that the majority of employees wish they had more flexibility built into their job.

I don't want to rub it in too bad, but I have the kind of work schedule that a lot of my friends would die for.

As I sit here I am writing this section from my home office looking out on the Great Smoky Mountains. It's close to 8 am, the sun is just starting to really show itself. You might say it is a beautiful morning. I've had my breakfast and am sipping on some warm coffee. My daughter is in the room next to me taking her time waking up by watching some shows.

Yesterday morning I went for a walk with my wife. That same day I was able to attend my daughter's very first singles tournament tennis match in the afternoon.

I imagine the kind of flexibility I have is exactly what the people from the Global Talent Trend report were referring to.

So, why am I sharing all of that? Because I want you to be jealous of my flexibility? Nope. Because I want you to realize that the kind of flexibility is something that you can have as well. Because guess what? I'm an employee at the time of writing this book.

The idea that employees can't have flexibility in their work schedule is a fallacy. Are there some jobs, like retail, where that kind of flexibility is really, really tough to find? You bet. But we live in a modern era where technology and the idea of work-life balance in the workplace is a real thing for many, many companies. My company has a very large portion of its' employees that work from home. In fact, they even encourage it for some people that live nearby one of their offices. Studies show that remote workers are more productive.

So, stop hiding behind the lie that you have to work for yourself to enjoy the kind of flexibility that you imagine business owners enjoy. Because it just isn't true.

In fact, most of the business owners that I know have even less flexibility than the corporate employees that I know. At least most of the corporate professionals I know get to stop dealing with work issues at five o'clock in the afternoon. Whereas, the entrepreneurs that I know never get to escape their work. They are "on" all the time. Sure there are a few entrepreneurs that I know that have a good amount of flexibility in their schedules. That is because they have employees working for them. But in those instances, those business owners have been lucky enough to find an employee who can oversee things when they are out. In plenty of instances finding that kind of employee is rare.

One of my own family's businesses is a perfect example. After my father passed away we retained one of the restaurant locations that he had been overseeing. Even though there was a General Manager, who is super talented and does a great job for us, running the day-to-day operations my father, while he was alive, and now my mother and I end up fielding calls from the management team on a regular basis. At all hours of the day.

The flexibility of one's schedule isn't limited to the workday. What about vacations? Do employees or entrepreneurs have more flexibility when it comes to taking time off and going on vacations?

You might think that business owners do because they can take off whenever they want. After all, they are the boss, right? Not so fast.

Sure, employees often have to request time off from their supervisors. I have worked for a lot of companies where that became tricky especially around the larger national holidays such as Thanksgiving and Christmas. Some companies I worked at even gave preference to employees that had tenure. Whatever the case, employees do indeed have to get their time off approved. But once approved most employees are able to go away on vacation and be completely unplugged from contact with the company.

I can't say the same is true for a lot of business owners.

In fact, just about every one of our family vacations during my father's entrepreneurial days involved business. Some were even scheduled in locations where he had upcoming business meetings. Those that didn't almost always involved a few phone calls or emails that he needed to take.

It drove me crazy that he wasn't ever able to really unplug. Sure, we got to travel to some amazing locations and experience some really cool attractions. But not because he was an entrepreneur. Because we did those same things when he was an employee and those trips were on the companies dime, not ours.

Wanting to have flexibility, or control, over your work schedule really comes down to the type of flexibility you want. If you are saying you really want to be able to attend your daughter's school event then I don't think it matters whether you are an employee or an entrepreneur. For the most part, because there are some corporate jobs where those opportunities will be limited. Or, are you saying that you want to be able to go on vacation without your email and phone blowing up? In that case, I think on average you'd be better suited to climb the corporate ladder. I'm not saying that corporate executives can easily turn off work when they are away.

Trust me, that wasn't the case for me nor is it for many of the executives I know. They take work with them everywhere they go. I know that to be true many of the folks that I interviewed. Take Anita Lane as an example again. Anita is a phenomenal leader and believes whole-heartedly that the company she runs is her own responsibility. That kind of mentality doesn't turn work off on a whim.

I'm saying that on average the typical employee stands a better chance of having the flexibility to leave work and stay unplugged. So, stop believing that only business owners have such perks.

Marital Status

When you are younger making a career choice is strictly about you. All of the factors that should be taking into account only have one variable. Which is how do you feel about those things. How do you feel about security, income potential, or even how people react to your title.

When you get married you now have another person to think about. If you are lucky and you choose wisely you will have a partner who supports your career choices through thick and thin. But you should still take into account how your career choices impact them personally and professionally.

For example, you might have a sales job that requires you to travel a lot. Some couples thrive on being apart because they feel closer to one another while they are together. While most couples I know don't relish being separated. The sales job that you have might financially provide extremely well for your household. But the tradeoff, the time away from one another, can lead to marital problems in some instances.

Travel isn't the only thing you have to consider when you are married and make career choices. You have to consider all kinds of things. Maybe your spouse is very materialistic and is motivated by money, title, and prestige. If that is the case then you picking a career path that doesn't bring those things to the household could be a problem.

I don't mean to put a negative spin on marriage. On the contrary, marriage can be a real blessing. But I learned a long time ago that going into a marriage is a good bit about putting your own desires and wishes aside if they don't mesh with those of your spouse. That is why it is so important that you talk about each of your careers before you commit to a life together and how you see each of your careers in the future.

Early on every single respondent that answered my survey about career choices was married. Literally, one-hundred percent of the people that responded were married. I thought that some of that was driven by the fact that most of the people were in the thirty-five to fifty age range. At one point only one person that responded was younger than thirty-five years old.

Looking at that group's answers, about seventy-five percent of them worked for someone and not for themselves. So, I assumed that the combination of the average age and that they were all married was driving the results towards more people being an employee, not an entrepreneur. So, I decided to push back on that assumption.

Sure enough, as I begin to talk to those particular survey takers almost all of them had always been an employee. Even in their professional life before they got married. In fact, those that admitted they had dreams of being an entrepreneur said that those dreams didn't show up until after they were married.

Can you guess why that might be? It was because being married and having a partner that you cared about and felt responsible for providing for pushed each professional to want more from their career. In some cases that more meant working harder in their day job so they could climb the corporate ladder. In other cases, it meant starting a side hustle business to provide more income for their family.

Here is the real point. There were no examples, no instances, of where a professional choose a career path because of their partner. At least not in the corporate world. But there were instances of where a person chose not to pursue a life of entrepreneurship because they were married in or in a serious relationship.

Let me reiterate what I am trying to tell you.

A person's marital status very much impacted their career choices. But not in so much that it pointed them toward one type of job or industry versus another. However, when choosing between being an employee or being a full-time entrepreneur the professionals that were married did not feel like they could accept the perceived risk of having their household's future relying solely on the success, or failure, of a business that they owned.

That is something that you are going to have to consider when making your decision about whether you are better suited to be an employee or an entrepreneur. But that doesn't mean that being married should stop you from doing what you want to do professionally. Because you won't be a very good spouse if you feel stuck in a career and are miserable.

Be in demand

The business world is evolving faster and faster every day. Skills that were in demand decades, and sometimes years, ago are no longer as necessary. During the hay day of the industrial revolution, there were more than enough assembly line positions to go around. People would line up for days just to get one of those jobs. But that just isn't as true in today's marketplace.

Some of that is due to the introduction of technology in the marketplace. It can be scary to admit, but there are entire professional paths that are anticipated to be replaced by technology in the near future.

One example of that is the financial advisor role. There are entire fintech (financial technology) companies that provide investment services using automated processes and artificial intelligence. Two of the larger companies are Betterment and Wealthfront.

While I don't believe that services such as theirs will entirely replace the need for people to have human financial advisors, I do believe that those companies and companies like them reduce the need for certain services provided by people.

A similar trend is occurring in the banking industry. One of the trends I have reported on in the past is that the retail banking structure is changing. Banks are opening fewer and fewer branch locations and are instead attempting to deliver their products and services more through technology. For example, one credit union I know is doing a large percentage of their mortgage loans via video chat. Their loan officers never meet the borrower in person. Everything is done electronically. I mean everything.

That is just two examples of how the demand for certain professional skills is evolving. A similar change is occurring in virtually every industry.

Keeping pace with the change in demand for certain skills can be tough. I once had a technologist tell me that if he didn't update his skill set regularly that his resume was outdated within a year.

Regardless, the demand for certain skills can play a key role in your career choices. In fact, I would argue that when you are making career choices that you should absolutely take into account the current and future demand for the kind of skills you have or are learning.

By no means should you choose a career path, whether as an employee or entrepreneur, strictly because that role is in demand. I say that because I almost made that exact mistake recently.

As you've probably figured out by now, I can be a bit uncertain about who I want to be when I grow. It's ok, that is normal for any forty-five years old. Right?

Anyway, not too long ago I was pondering whether or not I should go back to school for my MBA in finance or in a completely different area of study. The company I worked with had an educational reimbursement program and my supervisor was encouraging me to get my MBA. I was not so sure doing so would really help my career. Especially with the depth of experience I already had. Plus, in my mind MBA students study theory, not real-world application. But, if they were going to pay for it I figured why not.

At the same time, I have always been keenly aware of the types of roles that are in demand. Being a computer programmer has been and will likely always be an in-demand skill. So I got convinced, for about a week, that I should go back to school for a degree in computer programming. Not only did I see that as a move that would improve my job security long term, but I also believed, and still believe, those skills would help me in my entrepreneurial endeavors. Since just about every idea I have ever had required software skills.

The truth is that while ditching all of my finance experience and focusing on technology isn't a terrible idea what was happening is that I was buying into the hype. It was easy for me to find all kinds of stories online of people shifting careers into technology. I even found a story of a Harvard MBA student who taught herself how to program and ended up landing a prestigious technology role.

That could have worked for me as well. The problem is that I was letting the idea of how in demand technologists are that I was close to making a career decision based on just that one factor.

I want you to think about the idea of how in demand your skills are. I want you to think about what your career path looks like now and in the future based on the demand for those types of roles. But that shouldn't be the only piece of the puzzle you use when making a career decision.

Demand is important. But it needs to be just one more factor, albeit an important one, you consider when deciding whether you are wanting to climb the ladder or do the grind.

Time

This morning, like many others, our daughter said that she did not want to go to school. She had just come off of a five-day break from school due to being sick and a holiday. It isn't that she doesn't enjoy school. In fact, she is thriving in school. She is a straight-A student, has been accepted into Duke's Talent Identification Program and plays tennis for her school. She is crushing it on all accounts. Not to mention that she has a lot of close friends who she enjoys being around.

If she is performing so well and has plenty of friends then what about school could she possibly not like?

It is the structure she can't stand. She doesn't like being tied to a desk from 8 am-3 pm every day unable to control her own schedule. She doesn't like her time being controlled by someone else.

Does that sound familiar to you? Just mention the phrase "8 to 5" and most people immediately think of their work schedule as akin to being a prisoner.

There are a lot of reasons for that kind of response. The kind of work schedule that most employees face can be…well… soul-crushing. The typical schedule leaves very little choice in how your day will be spent. Many even have preset times for their breaks and lunchtimes. Depending on your job you might be trapped in a cubicle all day. As you move further up the corporate ladder more and more of your days are made up of a revolving number of meetings. I bet you even have meetings to plan for meetings. Have you ever experienced the phenomenon that can be summarized by the saying, "I survived another meeting that could have been an email". The t-shirt exists for that saying. Google it, buy it, own it.

If time is truly one of our greatest assets then it seems like a waste to have between one-third and one-half of our time dictated to us by someone else. Which is probably why so many people turn toward entrepreneurship. They believe that they will be able to own their schedule when they work for themselves.

I hate to break it to you, but that isn't entirely true. Remember my father's story? How he spent a chunk of his career climbing the corporate ladder and then eventually ended up as an entrepreneur? What do you think he would tell you about owning his time as an employee? I know the answer because that is one question I did ask him before he passed away.

My father would tell you that whether you are an employee or an entrepreneur that your time is never really something you completely own. As an entrepreneur, you do have more of a say-so in how you spend your time. If you want to close down the jewelry store to take your grandson to the lake you can do so. My grandfather did that for my brother once. But, guess what? No sales were made that day, so no money was made.

If you are an employee and you decide to take a vacation chances are that you will still get paid for your time. If you are an entrepreneur and you take a vacation you may not be making a dime during that time.

Age

I started my first real startup when I was thirty-six years old. By no means did I feel "too old" at the time. In fact, I wondered if it was too early in my life for me to be starting what I considered to be my first business.

Sure, I had started other ventures beforehand. Like I mentioned earlier, I was selling baseball cards back in eighth grade at the age of thirteen or fourteen. In between that adventure and creating GoGrabLunch I had done tried my hand at other ventures. That included a direct sales company that I am still a distributor for because I believe in their products and the power of plant-based foods as well as helping business owners with a variety of financial matters that I got paid to consult on along the way.

But, GoGrabLunch was my first shot at a company that involved more than just my effort. I suspect I felt too young to start and run a global business because even at the age of thirty-six my career was just beginning to take off. So, I questioned if I had the experience necessary to pilot our team to success.

You might be thinking that thirty-six is actually too old, not too young, to start a business. I know I've wondered at that point before myself. After all, starting a business when I had a family to provide for and a blossoming career may not have been the smartest thing I ever did. I mean, wouldn't it have been better if I was in college or freshly graduated with no responsibilities and I could live on my brother's couch while hustling away at scaling a high-growth business?

I say that because that is exactly the story I started telling myself when GoGrabLunch started to hit its first major growth spurt. Plus, I wasn't the only one making that point. I had advisors telling me that I needed to quit my job and go full-time. That sounded like a recipe for bankruptcy to me.

But, I did start to question if everything would be easier if I had come up with the idea when I was much, much younger and had fewer responsibilities.

The reality is that I was wrong. The reality is that there is never really a perfect age to start a business. Whether you are in your twenties or in your fifties, starting a business at any age is extremely tough and each age group has a few unique things they have to deal with.

Starting a business when you are "young," let's say in your collegiate or early post-graduate days often does allow you to be more focused on the business. Because you may not be married and likely won't have any children just yet. Whereas, many professionals in their forties, heck even their thirties, and beyond have those "distractions". I put that word in quotes because you know how I feel about using your family and kids as an excuse, right? Moving on.

Younger professionals often have not hit their earning stride yet either, so it could be that they can survive on much less of an income because they may not have some of the normal expenses such as a house payment. Granted they may still have student loan debt (sigh).

You could also argue that younger professionals have more energy than their "older" counterparts. I know in my twenties and thirties it was nothing for me to stay awake at night gaming or working on a project until midnight. Now, at forty-five, it is a miracle that I am awake enough to work on this section of the book at a whopping 10 pm at night.

If the young' uns have the freedom and energy to pursue their dreams of entrepreneurship then us older folks have something totally different at our disposal and even more valuable in my opinion.

We have more professional experience to leverage.

I've known people of super talented young professionals. But there is a reason that most executives at companies are older. It is because they have had more time to hone their skills and they have experienced much more in business. All of that adds up to some very valuable insight into the business world and how to better execute on a business plan based on that same business world.

I'm not alone in this point. In fact, one of the most

notable sources around entrepreneurship and startups, The Kauffman Foundation, found in their research that the average age of leaders from high-growth businesses is actually forty-five years old. They also noted that the average age of first-time entrepreneurs was forty years of age.

Clearly, there are outliers. Mark Zuckerberg and his co-founders created Facebook while they were in college. The founders of Instagram were in their twenties.

One of the startup incubators, Innovation Crossroads, that I have done work with attracts post-doctorate startup founders who are in their early thirties or late twenties. However, conversely, the average age of the founders at another incubator that I use to manage, Fairview Technology Center, is likely over fifty.

With the founders at the Fairview Technology Center, there is often a reason they entered full-time entrepreneurship late in their careers. It's because they had accomplished a lot in their early careers, gained all kinds of experience, and also had the discretionary income necessary to not only sustain their own livelihood but many were covering all of the costs associated with running their business. That just isn't a scenario that a lot of young professionals can afford.

So, you can see that your age doesn't really determine whether you would be better suited to being an employee or entrepreneur. Whether you are younger or older merely means that you will have tradeoffs you have to consider.

If you are early in your professional career you might have more freedom to take the risks associated with being an entrepreneur because you only have yourself to think about. You also might have fewer distractions fighting for your energy and time. But, you may not have the breadth of experience that many entrepreneurs benefit from. So, being an employee, for the time being, might make more sense. At least until you have built up your experience and resume.

If you are a seasoned professional you may have all the necessary experience and skills you will need to weather the storms of entrepreneurship. You may even have enough financial stability to be able to go long periods without sustained amounts of income. Or, you may need the benefits that come with working for someone else. You might want lower-cost healthcare benefits and matched dollars for the money you invest in your 401k.

The reality is that your age, on its own standing, isn't a good driver for either career path - the ladder or the grind. It is more a matter of the tradeoffs that come with your age and position in life at the time you are making those kinds of decisions. In fact, some of those tradeoffs can be mitigated.

For example, I encourage many of the startups I work with to establish a Board of Advisors that can help provide the founders with access to other professionals that bring experiences and skillsets to the table that the founders may be too young to have gained. Establishing such a Board is even a best practice in the startup community. This type of "brain trust" can also be set up if your business creates a more official Board of Directors. In startups that receive venture capital, this is very common. The Board is often made up of the founders and the investors as well as other professionals from key industries such as accounting, finance, etc.

With experienced professionals that are starting a new venture, they can sometimes offset the tradeoffs they have to make, such as limited bandwidth, by bringing in younger professionals to run aspects of the business.

The idea that your age, whether younger or older, limits your career choices, between working for yourself or working for someone else, is largely a myth. Some opportunities on either path aren't always available depending on your age. Your age might limit you to entry-level employee positions if you lack experience. But whether or not you choose to pursue entrepreneurship over being an employee or vice versa as your career path just isn't one of those.

Effort

There is a saying I have heard about entrepreneurs that is, "You eat what you kill". I know that is a bit crude way of making a point. But the gist of that saying is not lost on me. The point is that as an entrepreneur you can only feed yourself and your family if you make a sale.

Unless you are in a sales and/or a commission-only job then that is not necessarily the case for you as an employee. If you aren't in that type of role someone else in the company is out there making sure that the company has enough revenue coming in to make payroll. You should thank them for that.

What I am driving at is that one factor to consider in your career choices is the amount of effort that goes into your job. I know of plenty of employees who work very, very hard. Even those that aren't in a revenue-producing role or whose income doesn't depend on earning commissions. But without hesitation, I can tell you that running your own business requires a whole new level of effort.

As an employee, especially one with a guaranteed salary, it is a bit easier to allow yourself to be on cruise control. Sure you have to think about achieving your performance goals so that you get a good review and maybe even a good raise if your company does merit increases. Even if you don't get a great review you aren't likely to lose your job. It is people who tend to completely underperform that get fired not people who are just ok at their job.

As a business owner, you can't afford to just be ok at what you do. You have to excel. Which means putting forth the effort to excel on a daily basis. It means waking up every day with the mentality that you are going to go out hunting for business. That you are willing to do whatever it takes to succeed. Businesses fail for a lot of reasons. Some never identify the right target market, while others are undercapitalized. But a lack of effort, or a lack of effort around the right activities, steal just as many entrepreneur's dreams as the other reasons.

That is why it is critical that if you are thinking through your career options that you be completely honest with yourself. If you are the type of professional you has never really been motivated enough to put forth the kind of effort that it takes to excel in your past jobs then what makes you think that you can suddenly change that?

Just because you would be working for yourself doesn't mean that you are going to find the motivation to put forth the level of effort it is going to take to succeed. Assuming that you can flip a switch and suddenly become a workhorse is a mistake. I know of plenty of people who were average employees at best who went to work for themselves and thought things were going to be different. They got all excited at the prospects of being their own boss and wrapped up in the planning process of launching their big idea that they failed to be honest about their work ethic. Whether as an entrepreneur or an employee, a dedicated work ethic is something that you tend to either have or not have. I'll admit that it can ebb and flow a bit. If I am completely honest with you I'd say that my own work ethic changes over time. My personality is the type that goes through stretches where I will work like a mad person and accomplish all kinds of things. But then I eventually hit burnout and my work ethic dips while I unconsciously allow myself to rest and recuperate. With me there just isn't a middle ground. It has taken me years to learn what type of cycle is how I work best. This means that full-fledged entrepreneurship may not be the best path for me. Because, at least in my opinion, as a full-time entrepreneur who has to "eat what they kill" there would be very little margin for a down cycle.

Career Ceilings and Floors

One of my father's favorite sayings about climbing the corporate ladder was, "The higher up you go the closer you are to the door". His point was that the higher up in an organization you go the more likely you are to be fired. That saying came from his own professional experience. So, I am not entirely sure that I agree with the gist of his point.

Some people, maybe even you, would completely disagree with his point. You might feel that it is usually the people in the more entry-level positions that are the victims of layoffs or even of being fired when things get tough at a company.

Whichever side of that argument you fall you on, we can all probably agree on another point. Employees on the lower side of an organizational chart oftentimes feel like they are stuck underneath a glass ceiling when it comes to getting a promotion. Ceilings, or getting to the next or higher-levels of a career, are a real thing. There are plenty of reasons why career ceilings exist. The simplest reason is that the higher up you want to climb in an organization the fewer positions there are at those levels. To reach the executive suite at a company you oftentimes need to have a perfect mix of the right contacts, the right education, the right level of performance in your former roles, and even the right timing.

Entrepreneurs don't really experience career ceilings. Since they are the boss there really is no higher position they can grind their way into. So, if a title is something that you are highly motivated by then this is something that you are going to want to consider in your career choices.

I do want to take a moment to pause and point out something.

In my opinion, holding a Senior Vice President title at a billion-dollar company is far, far more impressive than being the CEO or Founder of a pre-revenue startup. Anyone can spend the money to form a company and name themselves the CEO.

Career ceilings can be about more than a prestigious title. Many of the people I have talked to that are driven by their professional titles were really seeking something other than a prestigious title. They were after the other benefits that come with those titles. Namely money.

I experienced this myself when I stepped down from the company where I stood a strong chance of being CEO one day. Many of the people I knew called me in shock when I had left that company to pursue a different career. I even had one of my very, very good professional friends call and chew me out. He just couldn't believe that I was leaving behind the opportunity to fulfill a lifelong career dream. The truth is that he couldn't believe I was turning away from the title and income that could come with that title.

The problem with that view is that we were both motivated by different things at that time. He was clearly focused on the financial benefits of being a CEO. Whereas I was making a change because I wanted more time to focus on the type of work that I enjoyed and thrived in doing (strategic work). I was already earning a really good income so I was more focused on having less stress and getting more control over my time.

If being an employee means that you are more susceptible to experiencing a career ceiling, then being an entrepreneur likely means that your career floor is a bit lower.

Let me explain what I mean by a career floor. If a career ceiling can be defined as hitting a point in your career where you have maxed out your potential for promotions, and therefore the benefits that come with those promotions, then a career floor could be seen as far your career can fall. Most of the people that I know who are employed by someone else have very rarely seen their career plummet multiple levels. I have witnessed a few professionals get demoted in my career. But, that is very rare. Those that are demoted often seek new employment. If they get fired or laid off the employees I know have often been able to land on their feet in a similar role just with a different company. But the entrepreneurs that I know whose companies have failed are often in a tough position. They still often land on their feet usually back in the industry where they left off their employment. Just not in the same level of position. If they were a manager when they left to start their own business the folks I know have had to re-enter the corporate world in a non-managerial position. They also end up having to rebuild their careers.

I'm not telling you this to scare you away from your professional dreams of entrepreneurship. I just want you to be aware of what you are up against. It is called the entrepreneurial grind for a reason. The world is full of dreamers who have been chewed up and spit out by running their own business. Thus the reason I say that the career floor is much, much lower for entrepreneurs.

Control

So far I have talked about ten or more factors that you should consider in your career decision-making process. Each one carries its own merit and is important. But, by now you have probably realized that some factors mean more to you than others do. For a lot of the people, I talked with the ability to express themselves was the key factor. For others, it was the ability to make money.

But I have a hunch that it all comes down to own all-encompassing factor. People want to feel in control.
Whether you are better suited to be an employee or entrepreneur probably comes down to the perceived amount of control that each path gives you.

If you are like most of the people I talked to and you value the ability to express yourself then you might feel that being your own boss is the only way to accomplish that. You might believe that as an employee you don't get to pick the things that you work on or even how you go about those projects. I won't pretend that isn't a valid concern. What I will tell you is that as an entrepreneur you don't always get to work on the projects you want to or with the clients that you prefer to work for. Because there are times that the almighty dollar, or the need to make money, supersede your desire to be creative. I can personally speak to that point.

I was once working on a project for a client that had appeared to be the type of project that would allow me to scratch a creative itch. By the time I was due to present my work to the client I was super excited about how things had turned out. But there was a problem. The client didn't hate the end result. But they felt it was almost too creative. Implementing the work I had done was going to be a real stretch for them. I knew deep down that it was the right path that would lead them toward success. All of my research confirmed those thoughts. But the client just couldn't get behind this new approach. So, I had a choice to make. Either redo the work to suit their desires, even though I knew it was wrong, or not get paid. I'd like to tell you that I had a mic-drop moment and told the client to piss off. I didn't.

Noticed that I said perceived control earlier. Because that is what it is. Yes, sometimes being the boss gives you more control than not being in charge. But, believe it or not, there are instances where being an employee gives you more control. You just may not see it that way.

In the next section, we are going to take a look back at the strengths of climbing the corporate ladder or the entrepreneurial grind.

Ladder strengths

I hope you have spent some time thinking through each of the factors I've shared so far and how you feel about them personally. Where do they rank in your list of priorities? If you are the type of person who values money above everything else that is ok. Just be honest with yourself about that. Otherwise, you will be miserable trying to be someone you aren't.

Each career path, whether the ladder or the grind, has its pluses and minuses. Now that we have looked at various factors that people consider when deciding on a career path, I want to try and summarize back to you what I see as the strengths of being an employee are.

I'm sure that there will be some disagreement, but I have to start with income security. Unless you are working for a company that is extremely small or insolvent then most likely your paycheck is going to clear the bank. Entrepreneurs just don't have that luxury. No sales equal no paycheck most of the time for a business owner. Employees, particularly those that work for large companies, don't have that to worry about.

Not far behind income security is the fact that employees may have some sort of health benefits that are partially paid for by the employer. In fact, the research proves that around half of the employees in the United States have company-sponsored health insurance. While some sources say that only 35% of companies offer vision coverage, that still beats the fact that entrepreneurs have to pay for their own benefits, which are often expensive in comparison.

Next, let's take a look at time off. At least when it comes to paid time off the employees have it. An entrepreneur can certainly take off more time than most employees. But time off for an entrepreneur can mean no income. A typical employee gets 10 days off a year, check in hand.

Each of these strengths of employment ranked pretty high in my survey. After all, we could combine them all into one main category associated with financial benefits or money. Remember, that money ranked as the second most important factor in my survey. But it did not rank as the top factor. That factor belongs to the grind.

Grind Strengths

Being an entrepreneur certainly has its positives compared to being an employee.

At the top is the ability to work on the projects that you want to work on. Or, as the survey categorized it - the ability to express oneself. As an entrepreneur, you have the complete and utter leeway to work on whatever project(s) you feel compelled to work on. Whenever you feel compelled to work on them. Certainly, if you want to earn a living, you may have to take on projects you aren't passionate about. But you still have that choice. Employees, even those at the senior executive level, don't really have the ability to be overly selective of what they do with their time.

Entrepreneurs also have more flexibility in general. Particularly when it comes to their work schedule. If an entrepreneur wants their business hours to be from three o'clock in the afternoon until midnight that is there choice. Whereas a huge chunk of employees works a set schedule, often times the dreaded 9-5 workday.

While running your own business you can also decide how much effort you want to put into your business. Assuming the business is producing enough income, a business owner can choose to close up shop and go home early. I have more than a few restaurants in my city that only serve breakfast and lunch. When I asked one of those restaurant owners why he closed for dinner he said that he didn't need any more money. Only serving the first two meals of the day allowed him to accomplish what he wanted. Beyond that, he just wanted to be home with his family.

I'd be remiss if I didn't talk about money again as it relates to being an entrepreneur. I haven't overlooked the ability of entrepreneurs to earn as much money as they want. Without question, employees have a lower ceiling on earnings. But, in terms of income, I do feel like employees win out versus entrepreneurs. I realize that my own findings show that entrepreneurs earn more on average than employees do. But I personally discount that some due to the fact that there are likely entrepreneurs who are earning massive sums of money skewing that average.

It is important to note that many of the strengths that entrepreneurs experience compared to employees are factors that did not rank that high in my survey. In fact, only one (the ability to express oneself) ranked higher than the strengths associated with being an employee.

Do Your Research

Simply going through the factors I listed earlier, and hopefully any other factors you can think of that are important or should be important to you, isn't going to be enough to help you make up your mind about which career path is best for you. There is still more work that you need to do to better understand what you are looking for in a career.

But, before we get to more things to think about I want to take a moment to acknowledge something else that is important to this process.

A person's career, just like life, is often not a fixed journey. The statistics, as usual, vary depending on who you ask for data. But, in general, you can expect to have between five and ten different careers in your professional life. However, those five to ten "careers" should probably be defined as roles or jobs since they are often in the same industry. In terms of how often people truly change industries, I didn't find any solid data that I felt was worth sharing. I suspect that most professionals don't change industries all that often. At most I would think up to three times in their professional life.

Using myself as a reference, I know that I have rarely taken the time to talk to other professionals who are working in the industry that I was considering going into. Instead, I jumped right into jobs based on my perceived knowledge of what the job would be like and what the industry was like. That is exactly how I got into the financial sector. Luckily for me, it turned out to be a good fit. But that wasn't because I took the time to learn about the pros and cons of the industry.

I don't want you to do the same thing. If you are new to your professional life, or even if you are thinking about making a change, I want you to slow down your decision-making process. I want you to do some research.

I'm going to talk about a few ways to do that research. From looking at your hobbies to talking to mentors, or even reflecting back on your childhood.

The whole point of doing your research is to minimize the chances that you pick a career that just isn't a good fit for you. Once you have done that research take the information that you have gathered and then compare those notes to the factors that you decided are important to you. Do other professionals that are already in the industry you are considering entering experience the benefits of the factors that you decided were most important to you? Do they feel secure in their job and industry if you decided that security is super important to you? If money was your primary factor, do they feel like they can earn a significant income?

Keep in mind that everything is relative. What I consider to be a significant income may not be nearly enough money for you. You might feel like nothing short of a multiple six-figure income is enough. Whereas I just want enough money to live comfortably and to be able to retire one day. Not really, but you get the point.

I'm simply asking that you take the time to slow down and be honest about the move you are considering. I've heard it said that Americans spend more time planning their vacations than they do their careers. I don't believe that statement is very far fetched. In fact, I believe that you could insert all kinds of alternatives to the word vacation and the statement would still hold true. To be fair, Americans aren't the only ones making that mistake.

When someone is starting a business they are often advised to start with the end in mind. To determine their destination and then plan the roads they will travel to get there. With your career choices, I'd like you to do the same thing. Decide where you want to be many, many years from now. But once you have that decided take the time to look at the map and plot out which roads you will take. Talk to other travelers to see where traffic tends to hit gridlock.

Hobbies Aren't Professions

I've coached hundreds of entrepreneurs. Most of my time with them has been working on obtaining funding to get their business up and running. Because of that experience, I can tell you that the vast majority of founders that I have worked with ended up in their given industry and with their startup idea based on their professional experience. Meaning that if they had a software background they end up creating a tech-based startup. Or, if they have experience in finance they end up creating a fintech (financial technology) business.

The entrepreneurs that don't create a business within their area of expertise are often creating something based on a hobby of theirs. Maybe they love golf and because of their exposure to that industry they recognize a need for a certain type of solution. That then turns into a business opportunity.

Creating a business based on your understanding of a topic and then bringing a solution to the market that solves a pain point around that topic is a great start to being a business owner. But, starting a company purely based on a hobby is a terrible idea.

Hobbies just don't make good professions in a lot of cases. There are a wide variety of reasons that is true.

First and foremost, a hobby that is turned into a business quickly loses its luster when you are grinding away at the business for fourteen plus hours a day. You might love playing video games. But, I can assure you that Tyler "Ninja" Blevins gets sick and tired of playing Fortnite for hours on end. I know that may be hard to believe. I mean, I know plenty of young boys from my daughter's school who would jump at the chance to play video games for a living. Or, at least they think they would. But running a business takes discipline and structure. It takes a high-level of focus. The minute you add all of those things to the mix a hobby easily becomes a lot like work.

One of my closest friends absolutely loves football. From the day he was born college football has been an enormous part of his life. In the past, he has talked about how he wished he would have pursued something in sports broadcasting or coaching as a profession. So, as a way to start expressing that side of his interests, I suggested he start a blog writing about collegiate football. I can't tell you how good his articles were. Even from the very beginning, his articles were both entertaining and informational. I quickly became convinced that he really had a knack for the subject.

His experiment lasted a few short months.

Part of the reason he stopped was that he had other constraints on his time. Just like all of us. But, I think if he were honest he would tell you that when he started having to commit to a regular schedule of content creation that it became more like work and less like the hobby that he had escaped to for so many years.

Another reason that hobbies don't make great career choices is that hobbies, or interests, can change. In fact, they often do change. There is plenty of rhetoric floating around the internet suggesting that you turn your passion(s) into a business. While I do believe you should follow your passions I am not sold on the idea of turning them into a business. For most of my life, I have been a gamer. As in a player of video games. In fact, that is my normal night time activity after I have had time with my family. That's right, I'm one of the old guys playing games where ten-year-olds regularly kick my ass. Damn their reflexes! My interest in gaming has never left me. But plenty of other hobbies have ebbed and flowed over the years. I use to love archery. For all of a few months. I was a fisherman for about two weeks. If you are like me, hobbies come and go throughout the seasons of my life.

Whether you are an employee or an entrepreneur I would strongly caution you to avoid picking your career based on a hobby. There are some professionals where that kind of career path works well. But I have met very, very few of them.

Mentors

I've had a lot of mentors in my professional career. Some have been my boss, while some have been my peers. Others have just been other professionals from different industries. I even count the authors of the hundreds of books that I have read as my mentors.

Each mentor has taught me something. Some have taught me things to do. While other mentors have actually taught me things that you should do. Either way, mentors can be an amazing resource to leverage in your career. The same is true when trying to make career decisions. Mentors can be a phenomenal source of information. Again, about which careers might work and which might not work for you.

When it comes to choosing a career path I would encourage you to have at least two separate mentors that you work to get to know and learn from. Remember, mentors can be people you know personally or just people who you study from afar via books or online.

The reason I recommend two separate mentors is that I'd like you to work with someone who is already in the profession you are in and someone who is in another profession you are interested in.

Even if you think you'd like to change professions, working with a mentor in your current space can be very enlightening. If you do a good job picking mentors to follow you might learn enough about your current industry that you come to the realization that it isn't all that bad and that you could possibly make a career out of that job or industry. It just may be that you aren't looking at things straight or you need to take a different role but in the same industry.

Those are the types of things that a mentor from your industry can help you figure out. I have to believe that, given you have picked the right mentor to follow, that they are working and succeeding in your industry for a reason. If they hate what they are doing then you probably haven't picked the right mentor.

It is important to also have a mentor from outside your current industry. That isn't just true if you hate your industry and are looking to make a change. It is also true because you can still learn a lot about how to be successful in your current industry by putting to use some of the skills that a mentor has in your current role.

The benefit to a mentor from an industry or role outside of your current profession is that you can use their experience to learn a lot about what you might be stepping into. Both the good and the bad.

For example, there have been multiple times in my career that I thought about stepping into the financial advisor world. It was the first job I took after returning from living in Japan. But the timing wasn't right and I lacked the skills to make it work. Further into my career I got to know an advisor named John who had his own firm. One day over lunch I told John that I had been thinking about making a career change to his industry. He was quick to tell me that he thought it was a bad idea. John made it clear that he made a comfortable living, but that he thought the space was too competitive in our city and that new advisors tended to struggle. John also thought that I should stay put in my current, C-level role. Years later, while thinking about opening my own advisor firm again, my friend Justin indirectly talked me out of it. The industry had changed according to Justin and the amount of compliance that came with the role made it pretty burdensome. Even Justin was looking to diversify his business outside the typical financial advisor role.

All of those people were mentors in some form or fashion. By spending time to get to know them and watching how they went about their profession I was able to learn that perhaps the career change that I thought made perfect sense really wasn't the best fit for me. Had I never taken the time to talk to those mentors I could have made the wrong career choice.

Who Do You Know?

If you have read any of my other work, which is typically based on my finance experience, or seen any of my presentations then you very likely already know that I love the saying, "Who do you know?". That question is my personal go-to in networking situations or when helping entrepreneurs raise money for their startup.

I can attribute a large amount of credit in my professional career to the use of that question and how it lead me to become one of the most well-connected people in my town at one point. Using that question is also extremely valuable when you are trying to determine the best career path for you to pursue. Speaker and writer, Jon Acuff, shared in his book "Do Over" that the relationships you have, in both your personal and professional lives, play a key role when trying to get through a career change. I couldn't agree more.

Not only have my own relationships bailed me out when I was laid off by providing me with job leads, but they have also come in handy when I have had tough career choices in front of me. For example, I had recently been looking at an opportunity back in the financial services space. That move would have meant a significant increase in income for me, but it would have also had meant much less flexibility in my schedule and I would have to commute to an office again instead of working from home. That tradeoff was one I was struggling to work through individually. Plus, I uncovered some very serious challenges that I would have to overcome within the team that would report to me. So, I turned to some personal and professional relationships to get some help.

The key to doing that is making sure that you are asking for help from people whose opinions you truly value. Don't look for guidance from people who don't understand your values and what matters to you or just want to impose their own values and decision-making processes on you. I also suggest avoiding asking career advice from people who hate what they do but aren't willing to make a change themselves.

When making career choices in the past I made the mistake of listening to just about anyone that had an opinion. But this time around I was very deliberate who I talked to and got input from. Surprisingly, their opinions varied around what I should do.

Some of my professional mentors thought that it should be an easy decision. Most of them wanted me to take the opportunity that would lead to more income and more opportunities to go back to climbing the corporate ladder toward a CEO position. I even had one mentor tell me, "You are going to have to work 60+ hours to turn things around but it will be worth it". She would have been right if I was as money or title motivated as I had been when I worked for her. But I had changed.

The best advice I got actually came from my most recent former boss. I had left his team to join another and had frankly regretted the decision. But we had remained good friends and I knew I could call him for advice. In his opinion, I needed to focus on the type of work I enjoyed the most and not the other factors associated with each opportunity. It wasn't that I had ignored that question myself, just that it took someone else reminding me to focus on that aspect of the decision. In the end, I took his advice and took the role that allowed me to focus on high-level strategic work.

Once when I was working on my first startup I was struggling with the idea of leaving my day job and working on my business full-time. Almost every one of my startup mentors tried to convince me that the only way to grow a startup is to be a full-time founder.

But, I wasn't so sure. I was married with a kid and would be leaving behind a six-figure income. Not only that but I was also the person who carried the household benefits like health insurance. Not to mention that I would be leaving an industry where I was respected and where I was probably at the top of my career game.

Looking back, going full-time would have had its

advantages. For starters, I could have been more focused on growing my business. But there would have been serious tradeoffs. Like the potential of bankruptcy.

I can't stress enough how important it is that you ask for and get advice from people that understand you well enough to give solid advice based on your own morals and preferences. But if you do have people like that in your life then asking "Who do I know that can help me make this decision?" is one of the best places to start.

When I grow up...

One of the things I wanted to do to better understand people's career choices was to use survey questions. On top of interviewing a variety of professionals, I also asked others to complete an online survey. As I dove into the research some really interesting things emerged.

For example, one of the questions that I asked just about every participant was as a kid what they had wanted to be when they grew up. I thought it would be interesting to compare the answers to the profession that people ended up in. But, as usual, I didn't really have a good answer to that question myself.

The earliest I can remember is wanting to be a karate instructor. That idea began to germinate around the time I started high school. Not when I was in kindergarten. Which is the age I imagine kids being asked the question of what they wanted to be when they grow up? I can still remember my daughter's kindergarten graduation ceremony where each student was videotaped answering that question. Each kid had an immediate answer. Whereas, I was fifteen before I knew what I thought I wanted to be.

Notice that I said thought I knew. By the time I was nineteen I was the head instructor at the largest martial arts school in my state. But by the time I was in my twenties I had decided to move on into the corporate world so that I could "put my college education to use".

If I was able to turn my childhood wish into reality, but then elected to go a totally different route, I wondered if others did the same. It didn't appear that way. In fact, of the people that answered my survey, not a single person ended up in the profession that they had named as a kid.

Most of the answers were professions that you could attribute high-levels of prestige to in terms of well-recognized roles. They included things such as being a professional football player, a pilot, a baseball player or movie star, an astronaut, a psychologist, and a nurse. Only one respondent, when asked what they wanted to be when they avoiding naming a job title and instead used traits to explain their future work life. That individual wanted to be a "human who can hold humanity strong and keep creating value for human life". What an amazing answer!

It's an answer that I think makes a point. As kids and even as adults we tend to define our career through the use of titles. "I'm an accountant" or "I'm a teacher". We don't define what we do through the use of traits or skills like, "I'm creative" or "I'm analytical". Therein lies one of the traps of our career choices. By defining ourselves with a title we almost unconsciously pigeon-hole ourselves into those types of professions. Granted accounting crosses all kinds of areas of business, but an accountant feels like being an accountant is all that they are qualified to do. Whereas describing yourself as being financially minded leaves you more open-minded to all kinds of career choices. If you are financially minded you could be an accountant, a banker, a financial advisor, or any other various professions.

Imagine if that same approach was taught to us as children. Instead of teaching kids to think about their future in terms of titles what would their future opportunities look like if they were taught to think in terms of skills or traits? How many more career choices would their mind be open up to?

I suspect this type of thinking is why the vast majority, I'm talking over 80%, of people that I surveyed did not end up in the profession that their childhood self was targeting. The desire to be a professional football player turned into being a banker. The pilot ended up as a software engineer.

I'm no different. I wanted to be a karate instructor. I even lived that life, full-time, for a period of years. But I eventually went into finance. How the heck did that happen?

I'd like to introduce you to Anita Lane, who you will learn more about throughout the book. Her answer to this question was particularly intriguing to me. Whereas most people that answered the survey ended up in completely different industries than the one they aspired to as a kid, Anita ended up exactly where she planned to career-wise.

Now you may not see the correlation. Because, as a child, Anita wanted to be a psychologist. That desire was spurred on by her aunt who was a psychologist herself and who Anita really looked up to. But, by the time she was an adult, Anita had shifted gears to first accounting and then later on the hospitality industry.

So, how can I say Anita ended up exactly where she wanted to professionally if she wanted to be a psychologist and ended up in the hospitality industry? Because that isn't true based on her title. But it is entirely true in the way she goes about her profession. The hospitality business is one that is very much rooted in working with people. You have guests whose desires you are trying to fulfill. You have employees whose careers you are trying to build while helping them maintain a certain quality of life, and you have owners whose businesses you are trying to build. If you don't think that takes the type of deep understanding of the human psyche that a psychologist has then I don't know what to tell you.

Trade-offs

I don't read near as many books as I use to read. When I do read a book I am actually more likely to listen to the audio version of that book. I find the time driving our daughter to school to be the perfect time since it is about an hour round trip.

If you have ever seen me speak at a conference then you have probably heard me recommend my favorite book of all time. It is, in fact, the only book that I have ever started over relistening to the moment I had finished the book.

That book is Essentialism by Greg McKeown.

The title of the book might throw you off a little bit. It isn't a book about becoming a hermit in the woods and foregoing all of life's conveniences. But it is about "the disciplined pursuit of less". It is about doing less but better and focusing on the things in your personal and professional lives that really matter. For example, the author tells a story about an executive he was working with that came to a meeting with seventeen different priorities as part of her strategic plans. Pointing out that it is impossible to work on seventeen separate priorities at once the author suggested that the executive leave the meeting to go reduce the number of priorities. She came back with sixteen priorities. A whopping one priority had been removed.

When you are saying yes to that many priorities in your personal or professional life you are really saying no to other things. Learning to say no to things is a truly powerful skill to have. Because by doing so you are allowing yourself to say yes to everything else that really matters.

What I am really saying is that there are tradeoffs that have to be honored. That you can't say yes to everything. The same is true about your career choices.

It is nearly impossible to make a career choice that will allow you to have everything you want. If you want to make a ton of money as either an employee or an entrepreneur you are going to have to work a lot of hours to get to that level of income. If you really want to work for yourself then you are going to have to realize that you aren't as likely to have really good health benefits. Unless you are willing to pay a fortune in premiums.

Life and business are full of tradeoffs. It just isn't likely that you will be able to have a really flexible schedule, with top-notch benefits, and make a very healthy income. Can it happen? Of course. I know of people who reap all of those benefits. But it isn't common. Don't let all the self-proclaimed "digital nomads" that are on social media convince you that it is easy to run a highly profitable business from the beach.

The real question is can you get most of what you want out of your career choice? The answer is...absolutely. As long as you recognize and are willing to accept the tradeoffs.

I feel like my own career is a perfect example of this point.

As I mentioned I had the opportunity in front of me to one day be the CEO of a very large company. That opportunity was going to come with a lot of perks like a very high income and great benefits like a deferred compensation plan. But the tradeoff I was staring down was that I would be putting in 60+ hour weeks. After a long talk with my wife and doing plenty of self-discovery I decided that wasn't a tradeoff I was willing to make.

That decision was also made easier because I found a role where the tradeoffs didn't have quite as big of a gap from that opportunity. The role I moved to still paid me well enough to be amongst the average income level of similar jobs at companies like Amazon, Facebook, etc. On top of a healthy income, I was able to work from home (working in pajamas all day is pretty sweet) and have a flexible enough schedule to take long breaks. But I wouldn't have been able to make that the tough decision to leave the chance to be a CEO one day if I hadn't acknowledged and accepted that there were tradeoffs to my decision.

The Real Risks

A lot of readers want to read fluffy, confident, motivational statements about how everything is going to be ok. That they are going to easily accomplish their professional dreams. Whether those are dreams of climbing the corporate ladder, creating the next hot startup, or starting a lifestyle blog that allows them to live in Bali and work from a laptop.

I'd love to plug all kinds of motivational quotes into this book to convince you that you should go for it, whatever "it" is. That if you want to be a CEO one day there are only a handful of key things you need to do to get there. That one career path is riskier than the other, but that you should chase those dreams regardless. But, I can't do that.

I probably shouldn't even write this section right now. Because within a span of a few hours I have watched two entrepreneurs admit that their businesses were struggling so badly that they may have to or did have to close down shop. So, it would be easy for me to feel a bias that the riskier of the two choices is working for yourself.

You can stop reading right now. But you might want to hold on for a few more paragraphs. I promise I'm going to get to a point that really matters.

However you feel about the risks of starting your own business the truth is that there are always risks. Even if you work for someone else. It's just that there are different risks depending on the route you choose.

The risks associated with being an entrepreneur are numerous. Some of those risks are similar to the risks of being an employee, believe it or not. But many are completely unique to running your own business. Entrepreneurship is a lot like becoming a parent. Just as my business friend Canon Pattillo shared with me there is no amount of reading about entrepreneurship that can prepare you for how tough it is going to be.

The first one I think of is the isolation that many business owners experience. They may have employees or even other co-founders. Regardless, it is common to feel a complete sense of isolation. In some instances, such as with sole-proprietors that isolation is a real thing. But in others it is merely a feeling of not being understood. You probably have read stories about how a professional decided to start their own business only to find that their family couldn't understand why they were doing it. One of the most common places to experience this is between spouses. Just know that your desire to be an entrepreneur is probably not going to be understood by most people that you talk to about your endeavor. That may even include your loved ones.

Next is the financial risk that entrepreneurs face. I know of entrepreneurs who stepped away from their day jobs with clients already in hand and therefore, revenue in hand. But that is the exception, not the rule. So, if you decide to start your own business you should count on it being a while before you are able to produce significant amounts of take-home pay. If you are going to be living off of savings that you squirreled away you need to assume that you may never recoup some or all of those funds. I know of entrepreneurs who used hundreds of thousands of their retirement account to start a business only to see it flounder and eventually close. They never got that money back.

Finally, there is another side to an entrepreneur that not many people think about. I personally love to hire entrepreneurs because I feel that they often have skills that cannot be taught. They are willing to take risks, they look for unique ways to solve problems, and they are flexible. But not every business sees things that way. If you leave the corporate world to start your own business but then later decide to try and re-enter the corporate world it may be tougher than you think. I know of entrepreneurs who have run into this issue.

These are big risks that you have to be willing to take as an entrepreneur. I like to say that there are few things in life that can't be undone. That no matter how bad something goes most things can be reversed or at least repaired. That is true of entrepreneurship. If you take the leap and find out that it isn't right for you there is the opportunity to go back to work for someone else. Although it might be tougher than before your leap. If you sink a ton of money into a business and aren't able to generate a return on that investment you can always make more money.

Don't get me wrong. There is a point of no return when you own your own business. I know of plenty of entrepreneurs who were forced into bankruptcy because they sank everything they had into their business. Yes, you can recover from a bankruptcy. But it takes a long time to dig your way out of that kind of bad financial position.

Even successful entrepreneurs whose careers I have followed for a long time have had financial challenges along the way. Take Nick Loper of Side Hustle Nation as an example. By all measures, Nick is a successful entrepreneur. But it took him a while to get to where he is today. In a post from January 2020, Nick reviewed the last decade of his business ventures. In 2010 he was running an online shoe business that was experiencing declining sales. By 2012, according to his own article, the business had rebounded. But he was still forced to short sell his house because it was worth less than what he owed on it. So, not only was his business struggling but he was having to sell his home for less than he owed. The good news is that Nick's perseverance paid off and his Side Hustle Nation business appears to be thriving. If you haven't checked out his work and you are interested in entrepreneurship I recommend doing so.

Even entrepreneurs who raise millions of dollars aren't immune to financial challenges. According to an article published on Wired.com, Sahil Lavingia raised roughly $7 million dollars for his digital e-commerce business Gumroad when he was nineteen years old. But the business eventually stopped growing at the rate his investors were anticipating. So much so that some of his investors tried to talk him into closing the business. He chose to stick with it and has learned to be satisfied with what would be called a lifestyle business.

I don't consider any of those things the real risks of being your own boss. The real risk in my mind is the impact that failure can have on your mental state. Because I've been there.

When my first start-up shuttered I saw it as a huge failure. After all, we had scaled to representation in 45 countries. I should have seen that as a huge accomplishment. According to some of my peers. But I didn't. I couldn't look past the point that we had made it so much further than most startups ever do yet we hadn't been able to monetize.

It took me a long time before I was able to reflect on everything that our team had accomplished. In fact, it took me writing a book about my experience. The title, "Lessons from a Failed Startup," alone should tell you how tough I took the experience. But the truth is that as I look back on everything we didn't fail. We didn't sell out for millions to LinkedIn but we had people across the globe that like my idea enough to become a client. That is something to celebrate.

You very well may not experience failure with your business. I pray that you don't. But the reality is that the statistics are against you. You have to know it's a possibility and be prepared for it.

If you work for someone else you have just as many risks. Many of which can be just as disastrous. An entrepreneur may lose their entire financial investment. They may even go bankrupt. But, if you think that employees are immune to financial ruin then you are mistaken.

Job loss is among the top five reasons that individuals file bankruptcy. Even if you get a severance package because of being laid off it often doesn't amount to very much. In my experience, severance packages are based on the time that you have worked at a company. Indeed.com lists the most common severance package structure to be one to two weeks of severance for every year of employment. Remember, the Bureau of Labor shows the median employee tenure in 2018 to be around four years of employment. In that instance, if you were laid off you would get between four and eight weeks of severance. Combine that with the fact that most people have very little in their savings accounts you have a recipe for financial distress. Oh yeah, that severance will be taxed by the way.

Losing your income isn't the only thing that employees

have to contend with when losing a job. If you are the benefits carrier in your household then you could be out of insurance as well. Companies in the United States, with 20 or more employees, are required to offer what is called COBRA health insurance options to employees that have been laid off. That type of insurance is essentially the same benefits that you had at an employee. But there is a catch. When you are an employee your employer is oftentimes paying a significant portion of your insurance premium. Once you are laid off you can purchase back your benefits but now you have to pay all of the premium. So, it can get quite expensive. Plus, COBRA coverage is only available for eighteen months.

So, clearly, there are financial risks for employees. But, I'll admit that the financial risks for employees aren't as high as they are for entrepreneurs. If you are working for a stable company your paycheck is going to make its way into your account and we saw earlier where the chances of being laid off are less than 3% across most industries. Whereas as an entrepreneur if you don't make a sale you don't get paid.

Career Options

I've spent most of this book sharing information and stories with you to help you make a career choice between being an employee or being an entrepreneur. But the reality is that this isn't a black or white decision. It can be very, very gray.

I say that because there is an alternative that I have only alluded to so far. In fact, there is more than one alternative.
Those alternatives have the possibility of allowing you to enjoy the benefits that come with being an employee while allowing you to scratch that entrepreneurial itch that you have.

Let's take a look at some of the alternatives that I have personally experienced or have witnessed other professionals experience.

The Employee

Your instincts might tell you to skip this section. After all, if most of the workforce are employees that means chances are that you already work for someone else. Or, if you are an entrepreneur, that you used to work for someone else and decided that employment wasn't right for you. I don't want you to skip this section because the chances are that you already have a built-in about what employment looks like. If that is true then there is little I can say that will convince you that working for someone else may not be such a bad option. I'm asking you to keep an open mind.

What do you think of when you picture an employee? Chances are you are thinking of a description that includes negatives. I imagine you are thinking of someone who wakes up early every day, commutes to work in traffic, works 8+ hours a day from behind a desk with the passionless zeel of a zombie, and then commutes back home through traffic to collapse on their couch after dinner.

Am I close to the picture you conjured in your head? I suspect I am. The reason I know that is because you are probably describing yourself. If not, you are describing someone close to you that does not like their job.

If being an employee is so bad then why does nearly 90% of the workforce put up with working for someone else? If it is such a terrible existence then why, when asked what they want to be when they grow up do most kids describe jobs that would mean they are an employee of someone else?

It could be because that is what most kids are exposed to. Because of the entrepreneurs that I interviewed for my SouthFound southern startup podcast series those who had a close family member that went the entrepreneurial route followed in those footsteps.

Here's a statistic that just might change the way you look at being an employee. In a recent survey, the Conference Board found that employee satisfaction hit a two-decade all-time high.

In fact, being employed by someone else saw all kinds of positive results in their survey. Here are just a few of the results that I noted:

- Across 23 components that impact employee satisfaction job security saw the biggest improvement
- Wage satisfaction for Millennials saw almost a 10% increase
- Workers commute to work was the most praised aspect of employment (see my comments below on flexibility)

Apparently, people aren't as dissatisfied with employment as you and I might think they are. Still, there is plenty of negative sentiment about going to work every day that floats around. After all the Monday blues are a real thing. I know I've experienced them. Actually, I tend to experience the work blues on Sunday. I bet you have experienced the same dread towards the upcoming work week as I have.

So, what it is about being an employee that leaves so many professionals feeling a sense of dread? Most of those reasons people feel that way come back to a lack of control. As an employee people don't feel like they are in control of so many things. Their time, the people they work with, the people they work for, on and on.

But the truth is that you do have control. Regardless of whether you are an employee or an entrepreneur you always have control. As an employee, you can always choose not to work at that company that you hate working for. You can choose to stop working for that boss who makes you feel insignificant.

You have complete control over it all.

Now, you may not like the outcome of those decisions. Leaving a job you hate without having a new job to replace it means that you could be hurting for money. Standing up to your boss could mean that you get fired or don't get promotions and raises.

Allow me to prove my points. Let's play a little game.

I'm going to name a few people. I'd like you to picture their career if you know who they are. If not, just take a quick break and Google them.

Ready? Here comes the first pitch. Jamie Dimon.

Did you know who he is or what he does? I tell you what, I will save you the Google search. Jamie Dimon is the CEO of JP Morgan Chase. He is arguably one of the most influential bankers in the world.

Now, is Mr. Dimon an employee or an entrepreneur? That's right, he is an employee of the company. He works at the pleasure of the Board of Directors. Guess how many of them there are? Eleven. Jamie Dimon has 11 bosses to answer to who can fire him at any given moment.

Mr. Dimon might have a bit more flexibility in his schedule than you do. But the tradeoff is that he has an enormous amount of responsibility. When Congress wants to beat up another banker it is Mr. Dimon that gets called to testify. I know, I know. But Jonathan, he earns a ridiculous income! That he does. He also likely works 24/7.

Surely someone of Jamie Dimon's professional pedigree could have easily made a living as an entrepreneur by now. But he didn't. He chose to be an employee. He chose to deal with all that comes with that, even in his early career. That was his choice.

Ok, now for pitch number two. Here comes the windup....Barack Obama.

Whether you consider yourself a Democrat or Republic, whether you think President Obama did a good job as President or not is irrelevant to our conversation. What is relevant is that the President of the United States is widely considered one of the most powerful people in the world. Now, someone with that much power is surely in control of their career. Right? Surely the most powerful person in the world feels in control of their career and choices. You already know what I am going to say, right?

The President of the United States, the most powerful and highest position in the world, is a mere employee. They are an employee who has one of the most stressful jobs possible and they make about $400,000 per year. Which is nowhere close to the annual income of a typical Fortune 500 executive.

But, let's put money aside. What about control? Doesn't the President have a lot of control over his or her career? Nope. The President has very little individual control over his career and job security. Even once a president wins an election they can be impeached. A President has more bosses, the entire population of the United States, than you and I ever will.

You see, being an employee does have its perks. Most employees work at a stable company where they know their paycheck will be good. They usually have some kind of benefits including health insurance and in many cases the employer contributes to their retirement through a 401k plan. If you have ever looked at your annual compensation statement then you know what I am talking about. If you haven't, then I'd encourage you to do so. I know that in the past my total compensation has been about 30% higher than my salary alone because of all the financial contributions that my past employers have made to my other benefits.

Entrepreneurs don't get those things unless they pay for those benefits themselves through the income from their business.

If you are an employee I am trying to encourage you to think about your work life in a different way. To take more responsibility for how you live and view your professional life.

It could be that employment isn't your problem. Heck, maybe even your boss isn't the problem. Maybe your beef with working for someone else comes from the bad choices you have made. Maybe you had to take on so much student debt to get the degree you have that you now feel trapped in the industry you choose. It could be that you have bad money management skills and now your expenses are so high that you feel stuck in your high-paying job instead of pursuing something you are more passionate about but that pays less.

I'm not here to judge you. I've felt some similar things. I'm simply suggesting that maybe you unwittingly played a role in limiting your professional options with other choices that you made and now you are blaming those limitations on your career. That car you bought you just had to have was paid for by income from your employer. They choose to provide you with an income instead of putting that money in the company's coffers.

I'm also not here to paint employment as rainbows and unicorns. I've had soul-sucking jobs that had nothing to do with me personally. Or, at least not much to do with me. I've had bosses who made my job so miserable that I had no choice but to find another job. I've worked for companies whose management acted completely immorally and unethically.

All that said, working for someone else, depending on what you value in a career, can be the right choice. Sometimes it comes down to which lens you are looking through.

The Entrepreneur

Entrepreneurship comes in all kinds of shapes and forms. On one end of the spectrum, there are people who start a Youtube channel and make a little bit of money through ads. Maybe they have a blog and sell their jewelry through that website. On the other end are the entrepreneurs of the world that solve the world's biggest problems and end up getting paid handsomely to do so.

Whether you simply want to create some additional money for your family through a side hustle or you want to be the founder of the next high-growth startup, entrepreneurship is something that a lot of professionals dream about. Last year the New York Post published an article that claimed that 70% of Americans want to be self-employed. The data came from a survey completed by Freshbooks, an accounting software company. According to their survey, around 27 million Americans were anticipated to leave full-time employment for self-employment during a three year stretch from 2018-2020. If that data holds true there will be over 40 million self-employed Americans as compared to about three times that many employed professionals.

Being your own boss certainly has its own mix of benefits and challenges. I've already talked about some of those, but just so we are on the same page I'll reiterate a few factors that add appeal to the idea of entrepreneurship.

If you go back to the factors section and look at the section where I talk about money you might recall that statistics showed that the average small business owner made about $16,000 per year than the average day job employee. Even if we consider that business owners have a lot of expenses they have to pay that employees do not have to pay we can likely agree that business owners have more upside when it comes to their earning potential. If you work in a day job where you have a compensation structure that includes a salary plus commissions and bonuses there is still likely a built-in cap to what you can earn. With entrepreneurs their earning potential is uncapped, assuming there is enough demand for their solution, their product or service meets the needs of the market, and is priced appropriately.

It can cost them, but business owners get to decide which customers they work with. I've personally fired a client before because they were too difficult to work with. The self-employed also get to decide the people they work with from within their own company. They have control over who gets hired and who does. Whereas, as an employee, unless you are a hiring manager you have to work with whomever your company hires.

There is another serious perk that entrepreneurs get that employees do not. While business owners do take on certain expenses that employees do not have they also have the opportunity to leverage the tax system to their favor. For example, they can write off certain meals and entertainment. They can expense the mileage they travel. The United States tax code has certain tax benefits built into it in order to encourage people to start businesses.

Entrepreneurs can choose to have an extremely flexible schedule. Whereas most employees still work the traditional 8 am-5 pm schedule, depending on the business the owners can work whenever they want to. Take video game streamers for example. Many of the people who make a living broadcasting their daily gaming sessions don't log in to work until the evening. Nor do they work a set schedule. When they feel like they have done enough for the day they simply log off.

I know that is a pretty extreme example. But as a small business owner you have the option of controlling your schedule. If you don't want to work any more than you currently are you have the option of not taking on a project. Sure, you will be out of that income. But, maybe your time is more important to you.

With all of those benefits come some negatives. As the business owner, you are responsible for making sure the business is pulling in enough income to provide for you and your family. If you don't work at that your family doesn't eat. It doesn't have a roof over its head. The same is true for any employees you hire.

If things go south that is your fault as the business owner. Which means you get all of the responsibility. Every bit of it. I know of plenty of business owners who have missed out on pay themselves because they had to use that money to pay their employees.

As with all of the career options available to you, the key is having a deep understanding of factors that motivate you the most and whether or not you are willing to accept the negatives that come with the benefits of that career choice.

The Intrapreneur

If you Google the word, an intrapreneur is "a manager within a company who promotes innovative product development and marketing". The original person that coined the phrase, Gifford Pinchot III, apparently referred to intrapreneurs as "dreamers who do. Intrapreneurs are employees who do for corporate innovation what an entrepreneur does for his or her start-up". But

I think of it in a slightly different vein.

To me, an intrapreneur is a person that is an employee of a company who leverages creativity and innovation to bring new ideas to light while keeping ownership of those ideas. Now, when I say ownership I am not necessarily referring to retaining equity in the idea or business that is spun off. What I really mean is that the intrapreneur is largely allowed to retain control over the direction that the idea goes in. They might also be allowed to retain control over their work schedule. You might say they have a high degree of autonomy.

Does that type of role sound interesting to you? If so, there is good news. These types of roles are becoming more and more common.

Personally, when I am looking to hire someone for a position I look for this type of professional. I like to hire intrapreneurs who treat their job like it is their own business and

I know I am not alone.

A co-worker of mine is a perfect example of an intrapreneur. Helanded at our company after a company that he was part owner at was acquired by the company. Today, he spends most of his time doing research, plus writing and speaking at national conferences. I've had the pleasure of seeing him speak on multiple occasions and I can tell you without a doubt that he was meant to be a professional speaker. His talks are truly educational but they are also very, very entertaining.

I'm also honored to call him a mentor. So, I've had the opportunity to ask him plenty of questions about his own career choices. Just recently I sought his guidance on a career choice of my own. During that conversation, he shared with me why even though he has had plenty of offers and opportunities, he has not stepped away to "do his own thing".

He admitted to me that there have been times that he has considered going back to self-employment. That he has considered going back to "the grind". But every time he considers that he starts to realize how great he has things as an intrapreneur. He gets to manage his own schedule, largely work on things that he sees as important for the company's strategic plans, and even reap the financial benefits of his popularity in the industry. The company provides him with all kinds of resources that would not be available to him, unless he covered the expenses, if he ran his own company. That includes amazing health insurance and a travel budget.

You might say that he has the best of both worlds. He retains a large amount of control over his professional activities like an entrepreneur while keeping the benefits that come with working as an employee of a large company.

If you are doubting whether or not this type of setup is something available to you, trust me it is. It might not be the type of role that you have right now or that you will have after your next promotion. Most of the intrapreneurs I know that have an arrangement like his are professionals who have excelled at past roles and have worked themselves into an intrapreneurial role. So, it might take some time in your career to get there. But I promise you it is possible.

Anita Lane is another example of an intrapreneur. Although, if you ask her, she identifies more as an entrepreneur. Even though she works for someone else.

I first met Anita during my years in the banking industry. We were both very well connected in our community and spend a fair amount of time at the same networking events. Our professional relationship became more entwined when Anita joined the Board of Directors at the credit union where I was part of the executive suite.

One thing that people quickly learn about Anita is that she believes in a "servant mentality". Meaning that she is very focused on serving others and helping them achieve the things they want out of their personal and professional lives. That is a philosophy that has paid enormous dividends in her career.

Starting her career as an accountant, Anita eventually ended up in the hospitality business. Over time she built up her resume to the point where, at the time of writing this book, she is the Director of Operations for a national, privately owned hotel chain. On paper, her responsibilities look a lot like that of a manager. Part of her job involves developing hotel managers and helping the company to improve revenue through sales activities.

Anita identifies as an entrepreneur because her role truly exemplifies the same qualities of what you and I might call a true entrepreneur. She has complete anonymity over her own schedule where she admittedly is on call 24/7 due to the nature of her industry. She also reaps the financial rewards that entrepreneurs experience by being compensated through a performance-based plan.

But, more importantly, Anita feels as if she already is a self-employed entrepreneur because of how she thinks about her role.

At one point in our interview together she told me that she has had her own side hustles in the past. Even more recently she had been offered consulting opportunities. Anita's response caught me off guard when I asked why she had yet to take the plunge into full-time self-employment. In her mind, the timing just isn't right. Not because she is too scared to follow her dreams, although fear is something she experiences when talking about what holds her back. Instead, she isn't quite ready to go out on her own because she has invested too much into the business she is running and she feels as if there are too many things left undone in the business.

Which makes complete sense. It is a business that she has helped grow for a single location to a regional player in the industry and the company's growth is only forecast to continue.

So, while I might call her an intrapreneur Anita's career is very, very much entrepreneurial. Her name may not be on the documents that legally list the owners of the company. But she believes and acts as if she is an owner anyway.

That may be semantics or even merely a change in mental outlook. But in her activities and buy-in to the corporate mission Anita is an owner.

The Freelancer

In 2018, Forbes published an article titled, "4 Reasons Why The Gig Economy Will Only Keep Growing In Numbers". That article quoted a white paper from Betterment, an investment robo-advisory platform, that said one in three US workers are freelancers. That number is only expected to grow dramatically. I know I have personally seen some articles claim that number will grow to 70% by 2025. In fact, I found that statistics while doing some research, as a freelancer mind you, for a Fortune 30 tech giant that was looking for data around freelancing.

The number of people that are freelancing doesn't shock me at all. Nor does the anticipated growth in the number of freelancers. Being a freelancer provides all kinds of benefits. I've personally been freelancing for over three years now. Most of my activity comes via sites such as Upwork where I am a "Top-Rated" freelancer.

I have no doubt that the reason over one-third of the US Is freelancing is because of the same reasons that I am participating in the gig economy.

First, whether you are part-time or full-time, the extra income you can earn goes a long way. My wife and I used my side hustle income to pay off almost all of our debt except our home. We also used those earnings to pay for our family vacations, make bigger household expense purchases such as new furniture, and increase the amount we have in our savings and retirement accounts. While paying off our debts has been life-changing, it is really the extra money in savings and our retirement accounts that keeps me going. In what feels like a short three years we have been able to use the extra money made from freelancing to completely change our financial future.

Second, freelancing has allowed me to scratch my entrepreneurial itch. Through some of the projects I have worked on I have been able to express my creative side as well as learn new skills. By freelancing part-time I have been able to establish processes and procedures for my business so that if/when I take the plunge into full-time entrepreneurship I have a better-developed business strategy. I am not alone in the part-time approach. A survey commissioned by Upwork and the Freelancers Union found that less than 30% of freelancers actually made a full-time living through the activity.

Another thing that I have always liked about freelancing is that it has allowed me to have a "Plan B".

I have been laid off three times in my professional career. The last time was when our daughter was nine months old. At the time that was a devastating event. Looking back I realize that we weren't going to starve to death. Because I wasn't going to allow that to be a reality and we had the support of our family. But there sure were days where it was rough. The good news is that I had a really strong network that I was able to leverage to help me quickly find another job. But what I didn't have was any other sources of income coming into the household. Not a single one.

If I were to get laid today I would still have at least three other sources of income to lean on. One of those would definitely be my freelancing activities. With the other two being income from passive investments such as real estate. I can't begin to tell you the peace of mind that gives me knowing that I have that income to fall back on. This is exactly why I continue freelancing even though we are in a much, much better financial position. Because having a business that is already up and running would allow me to quickly turn all of my attention in that direction to produce more income if something were to happen to my day job and primary income.

Like my co-worker, I believe I have the best of both worlds. I have a day job that is my main source of income and provides me with some fantastic benefits. Yet, I get to express my entrepreneurial spirit while padding our bank account. But, this path of being both an employee and an entrepreneur may not be right for you. You may not want to work all day only to put in a few extra hours every night. You may not like your job and just really, really badly want to strike out on your own. I am not trying to convince you that the way he or I lead our professional lives is right for you. I'm simply showing you a different road you can take. It's up to you to decide if you want to turn the wheel.

A Second Act

While entrepreneurship is a journey that can be started at any age, there is a reason that the statistics I shared earlier peg the average age of a successful entrepreneur is 44 years old.

At that age, most professionals have a combination of things going for them. While younger professionals may experience some of these benefits it is less common in my opinion.

First of all, they have a lot of professional experience built up. That experience allows them to be an expert in their craft. If it takes 10,000 hours of doing something to become an expert then no wonder that level of experience comes later in life.

Second, more experienced professionals have had more time to build up a network of contacts that they can leverage. Networking is one of the skills that I feel helped me the most professionally. Sure I was good at what I did. But it was my network, or more simply who I knew, that helped me build my career.

Also, more seasoned professionals may have more access to discretionary income that they can use to start a business with than their younger counterparts.

It is for a lot of those reasons that, in some instances, it is later in a professional's life before they decide to take the entrepreneurial leap. I call that it having a second act.

In the startup industry, you can find a lot of "seasoned" professionals who are experiencing a second act, i.e career. Generally, they are offering consulting services to younger entrepreneurs and they do bring a lot of experience with them. In some instances, they are later added to the startup team or they fill a seat on the Board of Advisors.

I am sharing all of this with you to get you thinking about the possibility of your own second act as a professional.

One of the things I have seen a lot of employees do that want to be an entrepreneur is that they rush the process. They get so disenchanted with their current state of work that they sometimes throw caution to the wind and jump into entrepreneurship with both feet. Only to land in quicksand.

Timing really is critical when you make that type of move. Sometimes it is better to bide your time and make the leap when you are really ready to do so. That might mean that you need to spend more time gaining the right kind of experience or putting more money in your war chest.

If you are dreaming of running your own business I know it can be tough to tell yourself to slow down. After all, half the fun of being an entrepreneur is the early stages of the business when you get to dream a little about what may be. But I can't stress enough how important it is to start the business off on the right footing. That usually means taking the time to really make sure you have a successful model in the first place.

So, maybe staying in your day job is the right thing to do while you plan your second act. Whether that second act is one year from now or ten years from now doesn't matter. What matters is that you put yourself in the best position to be able to succeed. That might mean waiting until the curtain has closed on one career before fully launching your next career.

The Best of Both Worlds

"You want to have your cake and eat it too".

Justin and I had been talking for about an hour about his current business and where his business was headed in the next few years. His business was doing well and it was time to figure out a way to step out of that business. It was time to be more of a business owner and let others run the business for him rather than running the day-to-day operations himself.

The conversation had somehow shifted to me and my career and businesses. Like a lot of people that knew me well in the professional arena, Justin wanted to know why I had never made the full-time leap into entrepreneurship.

I've wondered the same thing many, many times. Remember, that question is a large part of why I wanted to write this book. I needed to understand if I was better suited for climbing the corporate ladder or the entrepreneurial grind.

In the response I gave Justin I found my answer.

The reality is that I had spent years buying into the hype of being an entrepreneur. Or, as my former Content Marketing Academy colleague Ahmed Khalifa put it in our interview, the idea that being an entrepreneur is sexy and magical. That I could work from anywhere via a laptop and a cellphone while sitting on the beach sipping Pina Coladas.

That all sounded pretty amazing. It sounded amazing if the reality of being a business-owner even feel short of the idea.

But the truth is, at least for me personally, I didn't have it that bad. Sure I might feel the pull to walk away from my corporate job if I was unhappy. But I had a pretty sweet gig. I earned an income that was more than most business owners I knew, working out of my home, doing a job that fit my skill set perfectly, with plenty of flexibility built into my schedule. On top of that, I had my own side business that was providing me additional income as well as the ability to creatively express myself. Much to the point of the primary driver that the survey respondents focused on when selecting a career.

I had what appeared to be the best of both worlds. Or, as Justin put it "you want to have your cake and eat it too".

My answer to him didn't reveal the truth to me, it just reminded me of it.

After all the interviews, the survey, and then transferring that information into this book I had come to a realization.

Whether or not a person is better suited to be an employee or an entrepreneur isn't a static decision. There are times when climbing the corporate ladder makes complete and utter sense for a professional. There are also times that enjoying the ride that is the entrepreneurial grind makes sense as well.

Based on your personal motivations one path might make more sense than the other. But a fair amount of your career choices will depend on, as Ahmed had put it in our interview together, timing.

Stepping away from a promising career when you are the sole provider for a family probably isn't the best time to throw caution to the wind and leave that job for entrepreneurship. Unless you have a ton of money saved up and the skills to be able to successfully manage a business. Often when you are younger those constraints don't exist. You may only have yourself to think about.

So, what am I suggesting?

Whether or not you choose to climb the corporate ladder or experience the entrepreneurial grind is so unique to your exact situation that I can't tell you which path is better for you. But I can make a suggestion.

I propose you work toward a place in your professional life where you can have the best of both worlds. That you might a career that fulfills you and allows you to focus on what really matters to you. That means working for someone else while having a side business. The first will provide you with a stable income and benefits while the latter will allow you to express more of yourself and earn some additional income that can be put to good use. Perhaps over time that side business will grow enough to allow you to pursue full-time ownership.

I recognize that it is hard to grow a business part-time.

Plenty of the so-called social media "gurus" will tell you that you have to hustle 24/7 to grow a business. I disagree. In fact, I think the whole idea of "hustling" 24/7 is a huge mistake. The average person just cannot sustain that kind of life. Besides the fact that it is extremely unhealthy.

But the average person can sustain a full-time job and a side business while maintaining some level of a personal life. If you consider a schedule where you work nine hours in a day job, put two to three hours into family time each day, and then hustle at night for a few hours that leave enough time for other things.
You can have the best of both worlds. You can have your cake and eat it too. I know because I have done it for years now and so have plenty of other professionals. Remember, statistics show that 70% of millennials have a side hustle. You don't have to be a millennial to join them.

I started this book with the idea that there were two disparate paths a professional had to choose from. The ladder or the grind. I'm going to finish this book with this thought.
If one path on the proverbial career journey suits you better than the other, you can choose to be an employee or an entrepreneur. But, there is no forced fork in the proverbial career path. You can walk both roads at the same time. It all comes down to the life you want to live and the choices that allow you to live it to the fullest.

Research

When I started out working through this question, of whether I was better suited to be an employed or an entrepreneur, I knew that it would involve a fair amount of self-discovery. As I have grown older I've become pretty fond of taking time out of my normal routine to spend time asking myself thought-provoking, hard questions.

Some of that discovery comes in the form of brief daily journaling and then regularly returning to do a "journal audit". When the same questions or thoughts seem to keep coming up over and over, without any sign of resolution, I often turn those into personal research projects.

Which is how this book came to be.

Since the project originally came out of a purely selfish purpose I wasn't overly focused on what other people had to say on the topic. I did spend some time reading articles on the topic, but frankly, those always seemed to have a biased stance to them. Mostly in favor of promoting entrepreneurship as the savior of the average "day job zombie". I also spent some time talking to many of my mentors (see the Mentor section).

Then I ran into a problem.

You see, once I started opening up to people about the research I was doing I began to notice that they became really interested. In fact, many of the people I even casually mentioned the book to express that they were also torn between the two paths - the ladder or the grind. It wasn't long before I realized that this research into a selfish question was bigger than just me. That there were lots of people who were interested in what I was learning through my research.

With that, I had to admit that my own journaling about the topic wasn't going to be enough. If I wanted to share this information with other people in order to possibly help them with their own career choices I was going to need some external resources.

That is why this book includes not only my own opinions,

research, stories, and thoughts on the topic but it also includes the same from other professionals. I captured that research in two ways.

First, I produced a short survey that I opened up for anyone to take but that I also specifically invited certain professionals to take whom I thought would have interesting answers to share.

Second, I recorded live interviews, usually via video chat, with some of the same professionals that took the survey but also with others that did not take the survey.

Survey

The first step toward research, outside of my own journaling and planning, I decided on was to use a survey to capture as much information as possible as to how people make career decisions.

I went into the design of the survey knowing that people might already hesitate to take the time to complete it, especially if there were too many questions. So, I deliberately kept the number of questions under twenty. Without question, there were more things I wanted to ask people. But I decided to save those additional questions for the live interviews I was also going to conduct.

What follows is a list of the nineteen questions that the survey contained and my rationale behind each question. If you are looking for actual data from each question that is largely interwoven in many of the sections under the "Factors" chapter. Although some data is shared below.

1. What is your name?

I suspected going into the setup of the survey that people would likely be a bit more honest about how they make career choices if they could be anonymous. After all, for some people, it can be hard to admit that they aren't pursuing the type of career that you wanted to earlier in your life. Or, I thought they might be hesitant to admit it when money was the primary factor for the career path they chose.

To my shock, everyone that took part in the survey actually chose to share their name. Of course, that came in handy when I wanted to follow-up with a particularly respondent for more information or to include their story in the live interviews.

2. How old are you?

Here I gave respondents only three buckets to choose from. That was by design in order to keep their decision fatigue to a minimum.

The buckets were 18-35, 36-50, and 50 plus. I personally think of these in terms of one's professional years as early stage (18-35), growth stage (36-50), and mature stage (50 plus). Over half (56%) of the respondents fell into the 36-50-year-old bucket with the bulk of the remaining professionals landing in the 50+ bucket (33%). Millennials made up the smallest percentage at eleven (11%).

By asking respondents their age I was looking for correlations between that factor and the way they thought about their careers at that stage. For example, was I going to find that the younger group was more interested in entrepreneurship because maybe they had fewer responsibilities? Or, inversely, maybe the folks in the 36-50 range were going to show more signs of wanting to try out the entrepreneurial grind because they had had it with corporate life.

3. Are you married or in a committed relationship?

Exactly 100% of the people that took the survey were married. I would have really had like to have seen more diversity in the group. But I suppose that just gives me the chance to do more research down the line.

This question was important to me because I went into the project with the assumption that people who were in a serious relationship would likely make more conservative career choices.

That assumption largely held true. Although few of the respondents would directly admit it most expressed some hesitation to take the riskier of the two paths (assumed to be entrepreneurship).

4. Do you have children?

Two-thirds (67%) of the people taking the survey had children. Finding out the answers to this question mirrored my reasons for asking about their relationship status. I was convinced that people with children would also take a more conservative career path. That would end up another assumption that proved to be mostly true.

5. Tell me about yourself, in your own words

I left this question as an open text box rather than a multiple-choice question. That way respondents could answer in any way they felt. As I talk about in some of the other sections of the book, particularly the section titled "What do you do?", most of the respondents jumped straight into describing themselves professionally. Therefore this question served its original purpose in helping me confirm that people feel largely defined by their career.

It also served another purpose in that it helped me learn that I should have included a question on gender. I had left that question off the survey because I didn't want to allow any form of gender bias into the data. However, by leaving a question about gender off the survey I learned something important to the results. The one individual respondent who began describing themselves with personal, rather than professional, information was a female. So, while this question gathered interesting information I also recognize that I could be missing something important about how each gender makes career decisions. Again, another chance for more research in the future.

6. What did you want to be professionally when you were a kid?

I had to include this question. Because I wanted to see how many people stuck with their childhood dreams. I betting you could wager a pretty accurate guess. What was most interesting was just how far apart people's professions ended up from their childhood ambitions. Baseball players didn't become athletes or even sports announcers. They became bankers and insurance agents.

7. What are your hobbies?

If following one's passion is a good way to ensure a happy career then surely people would end up in professions based around hobbies and interests of theirs. But the reality is that your passion doesn't always equal your provision. In fact, only one survey respondent even mentioned business activities among their hobbies. The rest talked about the standards of family, kids, reading, and sports.

8. Do you work for yourself or someone else?

The survey was designed to get some of the more demographic type questions out of the way before jumping into the meat of what I wanted to learn from the people that took the survey. This question asked if people worked for themselves or for someone else. It also gave them the option of both working as an employee but having a side business. In this particular question, I was hopeful that I would get a nice mix of professionals. The results were great. A little over 44% of people worked for someone else, while 33% worked for themselves, and the remaining 22% worked for someone else but had a side hustle.

Which made the answers to the next question really, really interesting.

9. What one factor motivates you the most professionally?

This was designed to be one of the key questions in the survey. I was absolutely convinced that two things would happen. First, I was sure that I would see a more concentrated response to one, maybe two, key factors that people think about when it comes to their careers. Second, I thought for sure money and schedule flexibility would win the day. Neither assumption proved true.

The choices that people had were money, flexibility in my schedule, the ability to express myself creatively, a professional title, recognition, security, solving problems that interest me (aimed to test entrepreneurs), and others with a text fill-in.

Actually, the ability to express oneself won by a landslide with 33% of the vote. The next closest factor, or factors, was every other single choice with 11%.

10. Which factor would you rank as the next important after your above choice?

If expressing oneself was the key factor in a career choice what ranked second. According to the answers from the first question, all the other factors tied 11%. But when the participants answered this question there was suddenly a breakout. This time only three answers got picked. In order of rank, they were money (56%), flexibility (33%), and recognition (11%). Finally, my assumptions were appearing. But this time the factors that I thought would be a professional's primary motivation ended up as the secondary choices.

11. If you are an employee, have you ever thought of being an entrepreneur?

Want to guess the answers? Literally 100% of participants said that they had thought of being an entrepreneur. It is this question that I decided to really hone in on, particularly in the live interviews, in order to discover what was holding people back.

12. If you have thought of being an entrepreneur but haven't pursued it what has stopped you?

This was another text box response question that allowed respondents to type in their own reason(s). The answers varied dramatically. Suffice it to say that they could be summarized into fear, a lack of knowledge, and the need for a steady income.

13. If you are an entrepreneur have you ever thought of going back to the corporate world?

The choices were yes, no, and maybe.
This question was designed to be a myth-buster. I knew that most employees dream of entrepreneurship at some point. That ended up being everyone that took the survey. But I wasn't sure if folks that went the entrepreneur path ever wanted to escape back to corporate life. Sure enough, there were some. While more than half, 57%, said they had not ever thought of returning to working for someone else the rest of the participants either had thought of it (29%) or said maybe (14%). Combined I saw that as a pretty significant amount of entrepreneurs that had doubts about the path they were on.

14. If you are an entrepreneur and have thought of going back to the corporate world what are your reasons?

No shocker on this question. Again, this was a text box open question. Only three people choose to reply and admit their concerns about the need for money and safety.

15. If you are an entrepreneur are you full-time or part-time?

Those were their only two answers possibly. When thinking about all the previous questions and their associated answers I was starting to think that I was getting answers to the survey from entrepreneurs that were dabbling in running their own business. I was wrong again.
Eight-percent of the people that answered this question were full-time entrepreneurs.

16. What are the best parts of working for someone else?

Another freeform text box. Once again the answers varied widely. But one word did show up the most. Stability. One respondent even answered with a one-word response, "Friday". What didn't come up was any of the other factors from earlier questions. It seems that the mentality that working for someone else is the most secure path was impeded deeply.

17. What are the worst parts of working for someone else?

Remember how the responses in question #9 were evenly distributed once you got past the main factor of being able to express oneself creatively? The answers to this question confirmed how each professional seemed to have different factors that they hold important and without that or those factors they were unhappy working for someone else.

Answers to this question could be summarized into one word - control. They feel out of control when they are an employee.

18. What are the best parts of working for yourself?

Although questions 9 and 10 did not produce the answers that I had anticipated, this question sure did.

This question was a free-type text box rather than set choices. So, people had the opportunity to put down whatever they felt was important to them.

Sure enough, as I had thought earlier, money and flexibility crept into the people's answers. They weren't the only responses or even a majority. In fact, flexibility seemed to be the over-arching favorite. Not just flexibility in one's schedule. But flexibility in terms of controlling one's own goals and how they went about their work.

When money did come up it was around the idea of having no limit on the amount of money a professional could make. One respondent even said, "Unlimited upside potential".

19. What are the worst parts of working for yourself?

Businesses fail for a lot of reasons. One of those is a lack of capital, i.e. money. Without question the need for capital, as an entrepreneur, reared its head in this question.

The other theme was stress. Stress in the form of accountability to yourself and the need to achieve a balance between work and life.

To me, the desire for balance between one's work and

personal life seems to contradict the desire for flexibility.

It is virtually impossible, in my experience, to have complete control over your own schedule and have an utter balance between work and personal. With most of the entrepreneurs, I know the two are completely interwoven.

Interviews

When I started my own research I knew that exploring my own feelings about careers wouldn't be enough. Just as I suggested earlier that you do research about the career move(s) that you are considering, I knew I needed to do my own research. So, I decided to talk to people about their own career choices to see what they would share with me.

Any good researcher knows that the research is only as good as the information it uncovers. One of my biggest concerns was finding professionals who would be completely honest with me. It wasn't going to do me any good to talk to someone who was an employee and never had any doubts about their career. Nor was it going to help to talk to an entrepreneur who had never worked for someone else. I needed to hear from people who were in the same situation I was in. Who were considering changing careers, whether imminently or in the future, and who were willing to be blatantly honest about their concerns.

It turns out that finding people who were willing to be so honest was really tough. Before I invited someone to an in-depth conversation I was very deliberate about getting a sense of how they would respond to my questions. I did that through in-person conversations, like feeling them out at a networking event or looking at how they answered the survey. I didn't want to know all of the answers upfront and I didn't want to sway how they would respond. But I also didn't want to get someone who was going to feed me a bunch of fluff.

Once I had a small group selected I then started working on the structure of the interview itself. I tend to enjoy informal, free-flowing conversations. That has always worked best for the podcast interviews that I recorded. Over five seasons, or two and a half years, of interviews of startup founders taught me that my guests and I were much more relaxed and enjoy our time together if we just allowed the conversation to flow where it wanted to go. But, I also knew that I wanted them to expand on their answers to the survey.

I knew immediately that I wanted to record the interviews. Not only would recorded videos be easy to go back and reference at a later date but I knew that hearing the tone they used when answering a question would tell me a lot. I also knew that being able to see how they reacted to a question would be huge. So, I decided to use a video conference call for the interviews.

As I think back on those interviews I am struck by two things.

First, I know I picked the right people to interview. I would have liked to have found more candidates, but the ones I ended up with were perfect. I say that because they were very, very thoughtful with their answers. Nearly every interviewee had moments where they had to pause and really think through a response to one or more of my questions. You could almost see the inner reflection happening as they paused to think about how a question made them feel. Their honesty was truly a blessing.

The second thing that struck me was how much we laughed in our conversations. Careers and professional dreams that people have can be a very serious topic. There were certainly some serious moments in the interviews. For example, watching Jim Stoneburner talk about his recent move to working for himself and how tough it had been. Or how Canon Pattillo struggled with whether or not he was going to be able to keep his business open much longer. Those were very honest moments that neither of them had to share. But I am glad they did. Because by doing so they both gave each of us the opportunity to learn from their story.

The other interviews had amazing lessons in them as well. Whether that was how Anita Lane chooses to see her employment as entrepreneurship and how that drives her to succeed every day or how Ahmed Khalifa is content with what would be called a lifestyle business.

You can listen to the interviews over at jonathanmillspatrick.com/theladderorthegrind or read on.

Anita Lane

By pure definition, Anita Lane is an employee. She receives a paycheck each month from a company where she is not a shareholder. Each year the company sends her a W2 for tax filing purposes.

Even the type of responsibilities she has as more similar to an employee than an entrepreneur. As the Director of Operations, she oversees the daily operations of a chain of hotels across Tennessee. As well as oversees and manages the staff that works at those hotels. She would probably tell you that her main roles are to grow people and grow sales.

During our interview together I could tell that Anita felt a huge amount of responsibility for the success of the business she manages. In fact, her entire mentality was that the success of the business was her responsibility and her's alone. That sort of buy-in isn't very common with most employees. It isn't even common with most executives.

Combine that perspective with the fact that her paycheck comes from someone else's revenue and you might call Anita an intrapreneur, or someone that brings an entrepreneurial mindset to a corporate job. Which is exactly what I did. I called Anita an intrapreneur and I asked her if she identified with that categorization.

Apparently, I was wrong. Without hesitation, Anita claimed that she was an entrepreneur. She was quick to tell me that she was more of an entrepreneur than either an employee or the intrapreneur label I used.

Yes, the owner of the business paid Anita to run the business for him. Yet as far as Anita is concerned those hotels are her babies. As are the people that work for her. She had been with the company from a very early stage and had been part of the group of people that had grown the business to what it is today. Anita had been involved at all stages of the decision-making process and her input had been key to many of the strategic paths the owner had chosen to take.

It was a hard point to argue, whether or not she is an

entrepreneur. Her income did not rise and fall with the revenue of the company. She didn't own a single share in the legal entity that owned the hotels. Yet her mindset was nothing short of how an entrepreneur would address the running of a venture that they created. In fact, I have met plenty of entrepreneurs who showed less initiative and passion for their venture than what Anita demonstrates on a daily basis.

With that sort of business acumen and focus, I wondered if she ever planned on becoming a full-time entrepreneur. Anita had dabbled in the past at a few small entrepreneurial endeavors. But nothing had really stuck with her. She thought that perhaps one day when she had finally moved on from the hospitality business, that she might try her hand at her own business. But when I asked about the timeline for that she wasn't able to even give a guess. She was too focused on seeing her current role through to fruition.

I wanted to share Anita's story with you because of the lessons that can be gleaned from her professional experience.
What I learned from our time together is that, in some ways, a person's mindset and how they go about the work that they do can be just as defining as to whether they are an employee or entrepreneur. Just because you own shares of a company doesn't necessarily make you an entrepreneur. Nor does the fact that you get a W2 at the end of the year necessarily means that you aren't an entrepreneur.

Sure, by how most people define entrepreneurship that might be the case. I'd wager that there would be some entrepreneurs who would challenge the idea that Anita is one of them. But I'd be willing to measure her up against just about any of them when it comes to buy-in and commitment to the business they are part of.

So, as far as I am concerned you can be an entrepreneur, with the right mindset, even if you are a shareholder in the company you work for.

My interview with Anita also reminded of another lesson I had heard in talking with other professionals. The path to eventual entrepreneurship often starts by working for someone else, gaining a ton of experience and skills, and performing at a high level. Remember the section where I discussed the average age of successful entrepreneurs is actually forty years old? There is a reason for that success. These professionals come to entrepreneurship with a load of experience and skills.

I'm reminded of one other piece of my interview with Anita that I think is important to share with you. It's yet another reason why I think Anita can call herself an entrepreneur.

For as long as I have known her, Anita has espoused the concept of being a servant-leader. You could easily write that off as a necessary aspect of being in the hospitality business. After all, your job is literally all about serving others in that industry. But, Anita came to the industry with that philosophy. Not because of working in the industry.

It's not just some mantra she voices so that she is heard saying the right things. Anita literally lives and breathes the idea that as a leader she has to serve first. She serves her business owner by helping to grow his business. She serves her employees by helping them to grow personally and professionally. She serves her customers by providing them with a top-notch experience. There is no doubt in my mind that all of those stakeholders, as well as her family and friends, come before her own personal needs.

I can't think of a better example of what an entrepreneur should be like than that.

Ahmed Khalifa

I met Ahmed Khalifa when we were both members of The Content Marketing Academy. While that community no longer exists I do my best to stay in touch with Ahmed and a few other former members.

Ahmed was the community's go-to expert on Search Engine Optimization or SEO. He was and still is a source of inspiration to me for the work he does in another arena.

For some time now Ahmed has been sharing his personal journey of living with a hearing disability. He isn't completely deaf, but he is very close to it and needs hearing aids. Depending on whether there is a lot of noise where he is, Ahmed also reads lips in order to follow what people are saying.

During one of the Avengers movies, Ahmed realized just how difficult reading lips can be. Movie theaters don't show captions on their screens, so lip reading is essential for people with hearing challenges. With action movies like the Avengers, where there is so much going on, that is virtually impossible.

Ahmed shared with me how he left the theater that day completely frustrated. So much so that he felt a deep-down desire to share his experience. So, like any good content marketer, he took to Youtube. But one video wasn't enough. Soon Ahmed had started a second Youtube channel, his first talks about all things SEO and business, focused on sharing how life is as someone with a hearing disability. He is now, in my mind, a full-blown advocate for the deaf.

As an entrepreneur, Ahmed has been self-employed for about three years now. His story is similar in many ways to a lot of entrepreneurs. Ahmed spent his early career days working for someone else and honing his skills. But, soon he became disenchanted with being an employee because of the amount of bureaucracy and the inability to truly express his own creativity. He also disliked how the lack of flexibility of his schedule didn't allow him to be with his family when they needed him.

Based on our conversation Ahmed's business was doing fine. I would characterize it as a lifestyle business at this stage. It hadn't scaled beyond providing a reasonable income for just Ahmed. But, it wasn't merely a side hustle either. Which is very admirable.

One of the things I've learned in this process is that people's expectations of being an entrepreneur are often off-base. Many of them imagine starting a business and earning a substantial income. Perhaps they have read too many blog posts about making a six-figure income.

The data varies depending on the researcher, but the reality is that most entrepreneurs are lucky if their business provides the equivalent income of what they could earn as an employee. What doesn't vary is that most entrepreneurs are not taking home $100,000 per year. They don't even seem to have the flexibility that they thought they would have.

It's as if people go into entrepreneurship with blinders on. They make these vast leaps in the minds of what they think being self-employed will be like. But when it isn't anywhere close to that they wither away. Is that the media's fault for aggrandizing the topic? Or, maybe it's the fault of successful entrepreneurs who get convinced that any can make it since they did.

Maybe it is enough, whatever income level you are able to produce. Even if your business only ends up as a lifestyle business. Because that might be enough for you. It is for people like Ahmed and the reason it works for him is that he was honest with himself about how hard entrepreneurship would be. He very well may be able to scale the business to the next hot Fortune 500 agency. But if he doesn't Ahmed will be ok with that.

It is that attitude that inspires me.

Canon Pattillo

I very well may have learned more from my interview with Canon Pattillo than any other professional I talked with. It isn't that the other interviews weren't informative. But none of the other interviews left me with a sense of understanding as did the one with Canon.

I met Canon when he hired me to work with him on some research and financial projections for his startup, Inflection Learning. The business had been around for a while and was working on raising its second round of funding.

Inflection Learning was actually Canon's second startup experience. Previously he had been an early-stage employee in another venture that had exited and left him with enough capital to start his own business. But, things weren't going as smoother this time around.

The company was close to launching its first product into the marketplace. However, funds were starting to run really low. In fact, Canon needed to raise this second round of funding immediately. Otherwise, he was going to have to make some tough decisions that impact himself and the few other professionals that the company employed.

To say it was a pretty stressful time for Canon would be an understatement. You wouldn't have known it from the way he dealt with everything being thrown at him. Instead, Canon appeared to be the quintessential entrepreneur who was able to balance plates on top of long poles. All while keeping his sanity.

Or, at least I thought.

The reality was that the startup grind was taking a toll on Canon. Even though he had been one of the first employees at another startup Canon didn't feel prepared for his own venture. He had read every book about entrepreneurship he could find. Yet, he felt completely unprepared for the trials he had been facing.

So much so that he was considering going back to work in the corporate world. Canon was educated as a data scientist, so I knew that his job prospects would be really strong. That move would be one of necessity for Canon. Rather than one of preference. He really enjoyed entrepreneurship. But, he had a family to provide for.

Going back to the corporate world did not mean that Canon would be out of the startup industry. His wife, Alaina, had her own venture and was busy trying to scale it. So, Canon anticipated playing a role there on top of any job he took.

I wanted to share Canon's story with you because of the important lessons that I learned from getting to know him. First, his story reiterated what I already knew. That entrepreneurship is extremely difficult. Even for the smartest and most experienced professionals. But, second and more importantly, that the vehicle you use, whether entrepreneurship or employment, is somewhat irrelevant as long as you are accomplishing your professional mission.

That is the lesson that Canon taught me. His personal mission was to positively impact others. It didn't matter if that was as a startup founder or an employee of a company. He just wanted to make a difference in other people's lives. The vehicle he ended up using to make that difference was just a secondary factor. He could make a difference in his family's life by providing for them. He could make a difference in his wife's life by being a great husband and supporting her entrepreneurial endeavor.

I didn't immediately see where that trait had come from within Canon. There are plenty of fathers and mothers who can claim the same. There are grandparents who have given up everything in order to provide for their grandkids. If we are honest with each other, sometimes those people take on that burden because they should. Not because they want that responsibility. Not because it is woven into their core being.

With Canon that is just who he is. Maybe he learned to be that way in the military. But I don't think that is the case. Sure, being in the military probably reinforced that sense of serving. But it only reinforced it. It didn't create that mentality in Canon. He had served others as an entrepreneur. Now he was going to go serve others as an employee. Either way, he was fulfilling his professional mission.

Jim Stoneburner

When I interviewed Jim Stoneburner he had just recently launched his first entrepreneurial endeavor. It was going as smoothly as he had hoped.

A few months prior Jim had moved his family to Maine for what he thought would be an amazing opportunity in the financial services sector. Instead, the move and new job that came with that move had proved to be nothing like what he expected it to be.

That kind of experience is one I can truly sympathize with. When I moved to Japan I was sure that the experience would be life-changing. It was, but not for the reasons I thought it would be. I fully believed that I was grabbing life by the horns. That by doing something that most people would never do that I was "living my life" rather than just existing.

My reasons for moving to Japan had been purely selfish. Jim had made the move to Maine because he thought the opportunity would improve his family's future. When that didn't seem to be coming true he decided to correct course and return home to Knoxville, Tennessee.

The only challenge was that he hadn't had the time to land a new job. So, Jim took the leap into entrepreneurship.

It's a career move that he had thought about for a very long time. But he had never felt that the timing was right. Now that he had moved back home without a job already in place he didn't have a choice. It was time to start his own consulting business.

By leveraging his contacts, Jim is an expert networker, he was able to quickly land some business. Yet, not enough to sustain him long term. Which is why Jim was already considering returning to the corporate world.

Of all the factors that motivate people in their career choices security was Jim's top factor. During our interview, I pointed out that many people would say that by starting his own business Jim's prospects were less secure than if he had just taken a job with someone else. But the competitive side of Jim, from his days as a collegiate football athlete, wouldn't allow him to let go of the idea of taking a shot at being an entrepreneur. Especially when there were no immediate job opportunities in front of him.

What was most interesting about my chat with Jim is that he was only the second person, after Anita Lane, to describe himself by first mentioning his role as a husband and father. In fact, just like Anita, Jim's family was the topic of the discussion for about half of our time together.

Whereas some people see having a family and the responsibilities that come with being that family's provider as an excuse not to pursue a career path, Jim saw his family as motivation to take the risk of starting a new venture even though he felt that a corporate job was infinitely more secure.

That dichotomy was something I struggled with understanding. How could a professional view security as the most important factor in their career choices, believe that entrepreneurship is very risky, be razor-focused on providing for his family's future, yet still start a business that had few immediate prospects?

Then I got my answer. Jim is a believer and he had zero doubt that this family would be provided for, whichever career path he was on. In fact, even if entrepreneurship was only going to be a short season in his professional career, Jim believed in his core that what he was doing would improve his family's financial future.

That sort of blind faith was admirable and hard to argue with. I feel that way because that sort of attitude, the "no matter what it takes," is one that I live by. There is no avenue, no resource, that I wouldn't exhaust in order to be the provider that I was made to be.

That is what Jim and I have in common. It wasn't that he wanted to try out his hand about being an entrepreneur to express himself or to make his fortune. It's that his family needed him to find a way to provide for them while he figured out which career path he would ultimately pursue. His career choices weren't split down separate paths. They were going to be interwoven throughout points of his career and that worked for Jim because they helped him accomplish his personal mission.

Undefined

It really is a shame to me that so many people feel defined by their professional titles.

Take social media profiles as an example. I don't know about your profiles, but mine has almost always talked about my professional life, experiences, and accomplishments. They've said things such as "Strategist, Analyst, and former C-level banking executive". Or, "Entrepreneur, Investor, Financial Yoda". Yes, one of my friends once called me a "Financial Yoda". I liked the way that sounded so I took it and ran with it.

On a few occasions, usually during one of my many identify crisis, my profiles have started with "Husband and father". Those titles are truly my favorite two titles that I have ever or will ever have. But I tend to leave them out when describing myself. Why is that?

Like I said, most of the people I know feel defined by their careers. Which shouldn't be the way we live our lives. We need to live a life that is undefined by titles that other people use in order to measure one another's status in this world.

Instead, we should define our lives based on what we want to accomplish in this world. When I hear a child say that they want to be a veterinarian what I really feel they are saying is that they want to help animals. If they want to be a police officer or firefighter I hear that they want to protect people.

Professional titles are something that most of us aren't going to be remembered for when we are gone. But our impact on this world and the people we care about will be remembered.

So, let's take that and run through one last exercise.

I call it the "Gravestone" exercise. I know this will be a bit morbid. But sometimes tackling serious things has a way of forcing us to think differently.

Imagine for a moment that you have passed on from this life. If you had a gravestone, what would it say? Set aside the normal things such as your name, the years you were alive, and your family member's names. Let's think about what your gravestone would say about your professional career. Don't think about titles or money. Think about the things you hope you will have accomplished in your life.

This isn't an obituary. I specifically picked a gravestone to force you to keep your thoughts short and succinct.

What would your gravestone say? Would it say that you helped people meet their own financial goals so that they could retire comfortably? Maybe it would say that you saved people from crippling health problems.

Whatever career path you decide on, whether as an employee or an entrepreneur, I want you to start thinking and continue thinking about your career in terms of the contribution(s) you will make to this world. Remember, just like Canon Pattillo said, the vehicle you use to complete your personal mission doesn't really matter in the end. It isn't a matter of whether you checked that box as an entrepreneur or working for someone else.

It is simply a matter of whether or not you checked that box.

What I Learned

I started this project with some preconceived notions about employment and entrepreneurship.

In a general sense, I was convinced that being an entrepreneur was no less risky than being an employee. I'm not sure I feel that way anymore. What had likely skewed my opinion was that I had been through three different layoffs in my time as an employee. So, I felt that being an employee was just as risky as running your own business. I rationalized that no one can layoff an entrepreneur. Nor can a business owner be forced to close their business. But isn't struggling to create income the same thing? Being laid off, fired, or being unable to make sales all end at the same destination - a lack of income. However, it is really hard to look past the statistics. If most industries only experience, at most, 3% in annual layoffs but 70% of businesses fail then how can I tell you that running your own business is no less risky than being an employee? I can't, because you can't refute the statistics.

I was also convinced that being an employee was largely a soul-crushing experience for most professionals. But I came across people who were so mission-driven that they did not feel that way. I won't pretend that those professionals were the norm. Yet I can say that they loved what they do regardless of whether or not the job itself was a "dream job" and fulfilled a passion of theirs. Anita Lane didn't go into the hospitality industry because she loved the hotel business. She is passionate about serving others and has found a way to do that through her "day job". Canon Pattillo and Jim Stoneburner both desperately want to leave a legacy of security for their families. It doesn't matter whether the vehicle is owning their own business or working for someone else. As long as they reach their destination.

I am not here to tell you what to do with your career choices. My goal was simply to share some information with you in the hopes that you are better informed and can make better decisions with that information.

But I will close out with what I plan to do with the lessons I have learned through writing this book.

As a reminder, the initial reason I started this project was to answer my own question - am I better suited to be an employee or an entrepreneur. Life is never black and white, so I can't say that my career will be static going forward. Lord knows that my career has been nowhere near static. But at this stage in my life, I realize that I am best suited as an employee. I've had some financial success with various business ventures. But never enough to fully replace the income and benefits that I have in my corporate job and I am not willing to let go of that income or those benefits. What those ventures have done for my family is put us in a much, much better financial position. Plus, they have allowed me to express myself creatively.

At the same time, I can say that full-time entrepreneurship may be in my future. I can see that happening when my corporate career has run its course or I am so burnt out on working for others and we are in a financial position to go multiple years without any revenue from a business.

What I am saying is that for now, I plan to continue having the best of both worlds. To work for a company where I can earn a solid income and carry excellent benefits all the while experimenting with the side hustles that provide me with extra income and the chance to expand my skill set. Then, one day down the line, I'll likely have my own career second act.

What I learned is that this question, of the ladder or the grind, doesn't have to be an "or". It can be the ladder and the grind. There is nothing stopping you from experiencing both career paths if you are willing to make some sacrifices and accept some tradeoffs. It might be staying up late at night working away on your side hustle for years and years just for the chance at some extra income. But maybe, just maybe, one day you will wake up and that venture will have grown to the point where you are afforded the choice of the ladder or the grind.

Jonathan Patrick

Acknowledgements

First and foremost I want to give all glory to God for giving me the idea to write this book and giving me the patience to see it to its fruition. What started out as a way to answer a personal question that I was truly struggling with turned into not only a reminder of my love of writing, but it also became a personal mission to share the lessons I learned along the way that I pray will impact other people who are struggling with their own career and life decisions.

To my wife and daughter, you are the only reason I get out of bed everyday. What may seem as hustle and grit due to my personality is simply a deep down desire to make you proud, to provide you will all that have ever dreamt of, and to leave a legacy that will hopefully last long after I am gone. To my wife, thank you for being my partner in this crazy life. Thank you for being patient as I have worked through the balance act that is my desire to conquer the word while staying in my pajamas locked in our house.

To Chloe, I'm not supposed to put your first. But I lost that battle a long time ago. When you were born I prayed that you would inherit some of my strengths and none of my weaknesses. I lost that battle as well. I suspect that is because God knew what you needed more than I did. Very little brings me the kind of joy that being near you brings me. A close second is getting to watch you grow into your own person while showing signs of both your mother and my personalities. There are things that you do, intuitively, that baffle my mind. I pray that you will walk the fine line between being driven and at peace with your accomplishments better than I have. Good luck with that.

To my parents, thank you for raising an independent, highly driven son. Thank you for your unconditional love and being there when I had driven myself to a breaking point. Your persistent and resilience makes you two the original "Frank the Tank".

To my father, thank you for teaching me everything I would need to know to see that your legacy continues. Thank you for the silent career lessons that I lean on today.

To my mother, thank you for letting me hone my skills as your "financial advisor". I've enjoyed our game nights and growing the family business together.

To my brother, thank you for being my best friend. Long have our days of ruling the gaming world gone by, but our time together playing video games is what keeps me sane. Maybe, just maybe, all of that console-based thumb dexterity came in handy for writing this book. At least that is what I'll believe since it sure didn't help in our gaming adventures.

To all of my professional mentors that have poured into me, whether knowingly or unknowingly, throughout my career, thank you for teaching me how the business world should be and how it should not be.

To the people that participated in the survey and interviews associated with this book, thank you for your candid answers. I have no doubt that what you shared will impact others that choose to read this book. But more than that, I pray that by sharing your individual stories that you learned a bit about yourself along the way.

To you readers, I can't thank you enough for choosing to read this book. As I have already said, this project was originally meant for my own sake. That is why so much of what I share comes from my own perspective. But along the way I realized that I wasn't along in the struggle between career choices and dreams. So, I knew I had to share what I had learned with the world. I know that there are imperfections with my work. In particular, I would have liked to have more participants in the survey and interviews. I only hope that you will take my effort for what it is and that the lessons in this book are valuable enough to help steer you in your own career decisions.